What church leaders say about Alpha

'What Alpha has to offer is a unique mixture of Christian content and Christian style. It isn't only about communicating what Christians believe; it communicates it in a way that becomes part of the message, showing how the teaching leads to a way of living, through friendship and hospitality. I recommend it to all the Christian family in these parts as a very special tool of evangelism.'

Rowan Williams
Archbishop of Canterbury

'I think it is superb. I recommend it wholeheartedly.'

George Carey
Former Archbishop of Canterbury

'Alpha . . . a clear way into Christian faith for a wide variety of people. I warmly and heartily commend the Alpha courses.'

David Hope
Archbishop of York

'The Alpha course has spread throughout the world . . . It has brought new life to the faith of those who, for one reason or another, have strayed from the church after being baptised into it as infants. It has also brought joy to believers. In the United Kingdom there are reports that it has produced astonishing results in prisons and other institutions. We think of it as a new missionary tool that can be used by anyone, anywhere. . . We pronounce God's blessing upon the Alpha course in the catholic church.'

Peter Sei-ichi Shirayanagi
Emeritus Archbishop of Tokyo

'News of Alpha has been spreading fast and many churches – my own included – are becoming eager to learn more of its content and method, and of what Alpha might do in energising the life and mission of our parishes.'

Cardinal Thomas Williams
Archbishop of Wellington

'Alpha courses have brought many people to a living faith in Jesus Christ, and through these courses others have found a new dimension to Christian believing and belonging. I commend Alpha as one of the most exciting ventures in evangelism and basic Christian nurture in recent years. Alpha lays foundations in Christian understanding and discipleship.'

John Neill
Archbishop of Dublin

'I recognise the value of the Alpha course in helping people explore and strengthen their faith. I warmly commend it.'

The late Brian Davis
Former Archbishop of New Zealand

'The Alpha course has been used in many countries throughout the world and has proved to be a most effective tool of evangelisation. It gives us practical ways of sharing our faith with others: with those who have never heard of Christ, with those who have fallen away from faith, with those who wish to grow into a deeper personal relationship with Christ and his church.'

Most Revd Adam Exner
Archbishop of Vancouver

'Alpha is well and truly established in Sydney (indeed Australia-wide). Many have found their participation life changing.'

The Most Revd R. H. Goodhew
Archbishop of Sydney

'This is what I understand Alpha to be about: to know about Jesus in order that I may know him and the power of his resurrection.'

Walter P. K. Makhulu
Archbishop of Central Africa

'Today God is using the Alpha course to bring thousands of unchurched people to himself. I rejoice to see Alpha spreading like wild fire, rekindling the passion for the perishing in the hearts of countless Christians. My prayer is that our churches will not bypass such a gift from God for our generation. I would strongly encourage churches to discover the exciting effectiveness of Alpha. New life, in more than one sense, begins with Alpha!'

Moses Tay
Archbishop of South East Asia

'I am an unequivocal lover of – and am hugely thankful in my prayers for – the work Alpha has done and is doing. I am amazed by its progress in prison. I thank God particularly for the evidence of the refreshed student work.'

Richard Chartres
Bishop of London

'A growing number of parishes are conducting Alpha courses and I have seen for myself how dramatically and excitingly these courses are bearing fruit. They are bringing people into a living and active faith, and I strongly commend them.'

Simon Barrington-Ward
Former Bishop of Coventry

'The Alpha programme has in recent years caught the imagination of a wide range of Christians. For some it has been their first contact with Christ and the faith of Christians; for others it has presented an opportunity to reconnect with their Christian faith after a period of alienation or indifference.

There is important teaching about Christ and his church, not included in the Alpha programme, which the Catholic tradition would wish to add. However, I would like to commend Alpha for laying vital foundations on which others can build.'

Christopher Budd
Bishop of Plymouth

'I am very pleased to write about the Alpha course. We live in a time when the majority of the population knows little or nothing of Christian beliefs or Christian values. The great strength of the Alpha course is that it allows genuine enquirers to take time in exploring Christian beliefs and Christian values, while building relationships with members of the church. God is using this course to lead many people to faith in Christ, to active membership of his church and to know the power of the Holy Spirit. I warmly commend it.'

Graham Cray
Bishop of Maidstone

'Alpha allows the doubters to doubt and the seekers to find the truth. It provides an enjoyable and supportive atmosphere in which to tackle the great questions of life.'

Graham Dow
Bishop of Carlisle

'Alpha is fast proving to be an important part of the ministry through the church, especially these days when there is so much doubt and uncertainty in the minds of many people, even believers.'

Z. W. Gill
Bishop for the Kimberley and Bloemfontein District, South Africa

'. . .this course's beginning is orientated towards warming the faith of baptised people and then goes beyond that to the unbaptised. If Alpha does for us what it has done in other places, we are richly blessed.'

Richard F. Grein
Bishop of New York

'We want to evangelise but we don't seem to have found quite the right method. I think that the Alpha course offers easily the best method so far invented. I think Alpha is very successful because it answers the questions that people are asking today. It is user-friendly. It is not a confrontational course. It is presented in everyday language. It is compelling, but no one is pressurised. Above all, it enables us to come to know the Lord Jesus.'

Ambrose Griffiths, OSB
Bishop of Hexham and Newcastle Diocese

'My Anglican friends in England are very enthusiastic about the Alpha conference. At a time when many are seeking spiritual formation in the context of congregational life, the Alpha conference format has the potential to meet those expectations.'

Ronald H. Haines
Bishop of Washington

'The Alpha courses are transforming churches all across Britain, showing extraordinary success in stimulating interest . . . and then real faith among the uninterested and unchurched. I am so pleased to learn the courses are being introduced to the American and Canadian churches as well. A must for anyone serious about bringing others to Christ.'

John W. Howe
Bishop of Central Florida

'Alpha is a gift from God in mission today. Its simple structure – teaching, friendship and eating together – is borrowed from the ministry of Jesus. No wonder it works.'

Graham James
Bishop of Norwich

'The Alpha course is a valuable contribution to our commitment to evangelism as we move towards the new millennium.'

The Rt Revd David Konstant
Bishop of Leeds

'I welcome the introduction of the Alpha conferences into the church in the United States. These conferences combine sound teaching, personal experience of Christian community, and commitment to life in the faith and will be a welcome addition to the process of renewing the church.'

Peter James Lee
Bishop of Virginia

'Alpha has proved itself to be an effective way of exploring faith and deepening commitment to Jesus as Lord. I commend it warmly.'

Nigel McCulloch
Bishop of Wakefield, Chairman of the Decade of Evangelism

'Alpha courses are not only bringing many new people to faith in Jesus Christ, but revitalising the lives of church members, who are discovering the limitless resources of the Holy Spirit. The Alpha course is thoroughly practical, earthed to many of the key issues that all of us face. I see it as one of the most significant ways in which God is bringing fresh dynamism and vision to the church.'

John Perry
Bishop of Chelmsford

'One of the most encouraging developments in evangelism in the UK during the last few years has been the growth and obvious effectiveness of the Alpha group approach. It combines shape and purposefulness with great flexibility in use and we have seen it used in our diocese in churches of very different flavours. I am happy to commend it.'

Gavin Reid
Former Bishop of Maidstone

'I am regularly commending the Alpha initiatives to parishes because I have seen the lasting growth and renewal where they have been used.'

Michael Turnbull
Bishop of Durham

'The Alpha courses, with their emphasis on the basics of the Christian faith, are meeting the needs of many who are currently searching for meaning in life.'

Roy Warke
Bishop of Cork, Cloyne and Ross

'The Alpha course is a most engaging way of passing on the basics of Christianity. It is a tool for evangelism and nurture that I highly recommend.'

J. I. Packer
Professor of Theology, Regent College, Vancouver

'I believe that Alpha may well be God's instrument for salvation for many in this generation, just as Billy Graham was for so many in the previous one.'

Howard Marshall
Professor of New Testament Exegesis, University of Aberdeen

'At the heart of the gospel is both evangelism and discipleship. Alpha courses are designed to do both effectively. We have used the programme in our local church with good success. I am glad to commend it.'

Gordon D. Fee
Professor of New Testament and Dean of Faculty, Regent College,
Vancouver, Canada

'The Alpha course has now become one of the most reliable and important means of drawing people into the church and energising the faith of those who are already Christians. I strongly commend this to all church leaders and congregations who are looking for ways of expanding or consolidating their ministries. Although the approach was pioneered in London, England, it can easily be adapted to anywhere in the western hemisphere. It has enormous potential.'

Alister McGrath
Wycliffe Hall, Oxford and Regent College, Vancouver

'The Alpha course is a wonderful and proven tool for evangelism in the local church, especially in main-line denominations. I enthusiastically support and recommend Alpha.'

C. Peter Wagner
Chancellor, Wagner Leadership Institute

'The Alpha course is intelligent, biblically based, and incredibly interesting. I am convinced that when historians look back on the last few years of church history in the twentieth century they will have to acknowledge that the Alpha course became a significant instrument in bringing thoughtful people to a faith in Christ and into the church. For the inquiring mind, there is nothing better around than the Alpha course.'

Tony Campolo
Professor of Sociology, Eastern College, Pennsylvania

'The fastest-growing adult education programme in the country.'

Lyle E. Schaller
Church Analyst

'I highly recommend the Alpha course to everyone interested in discovering how the Christian faith can be exciting and life-changing in the modern world. The course is biblically sound, understandable, and practical. It will have a significant impact on people's lives and it will strengthen every church in which it is held.'

Wayne Grudem
Professor of Biblical and Systematic Theology,
Trinity International University, Deerfield, Illinois

'Every lively church needs a maternity ward! It needs a setting in which new Christians can be made and Christians can be made new. The Alpha course has proved itself to be a marvellous vehicle for this purpose, and it can be adapted to a very wide variety of cultures. In Britain it is proving to be one of the most effective evangelistic agencies at present, and it is something that any local church can run with proper training and encouragement.'

Michael Green and Michael Marshall
Advisors in Evangelism to the Archbishops of Canterbury and York

'Alpha has pioneered a way of doing evangelism in which people are exposed both to the truths of the gospel and the power of the Spirit. Here at last is a means of communicating the gospel which does not divorce Word and Spirit.'

Mark Stibbe
Lecturer in New Testament at Sheffield University

'For the first time I have seen a programme which embodies all of the principles which many of us involved in teaching evangelism have been expounding. I am delighted that the Alpha course is coming to North America. It is making an enormous impact in the UK, being acclaimed by churches of wide-ranging traditions, as well as submitted to scrutiny in evaluating the results. As our culture becomes increasingly secularised, the insights embodied in the Alpha course will be especially appropriate.'

Eddie Gibbs
Professor of World Mission, Fuller Institute of Theology

'I have been thrilled at the natural, winsome way Alpha has reached people, not least in my own family.'

John Goldingay
Former Principal, St John's College, Nottingham

'The phenomenal growth of Alpha courses is showing the church that we do not need to be defensive about our faith, but can expect people to be interested, and then radically changed by the gospel.'

Elaine Storkey
The Institute for Contemporary Christianity

'Nothing is more apparent to me than the blessing of God on HTB and the Alpha course. It has crossed my mind that perhaps God wanted to put his seal on the Alpha course by making HTB the British fountain-head for the extraordinary blessing of the Holy Spirit on so many churches nowadays. If so, what greater endorsement can one want! In any case, the blessing of God is on the Alpha course and I praise God for it.'

Dr R. T. Kendall
Former Pastor, Westminster Chapel

'We applaud the vision and work of Alpha.'

Bill Hybels
Senior Pastor, Willow Creek Community Church

'It's great to see how Alpha has been used to reach people who wouldn't normally come to church with the good news of Jesus Christ. This resource is very complementary to helping seekers connect with *The Purpose Driven Life*.'

Rick Warren
Author and Pastor of Saddleback Church, California

'Alpha is definitely a powerful tool for reaching the lost for Christ and helping them mature in their faith.'

Bill Bright
Founder of Campus Crusade for Christ

'I know of many people whose lives have been transformed through the Alpha course. I rejoice at how God is using it so powerfully to renew many churches both inside and outside prison walls.'

Charles W. Colson
Prison Fellowship Ministries

'Alpha courses are helping to change the face of the church in the UK. Throughout the country churches are catching on to a new and fresh approach to evangelism and the nurture of new believers. From small beginnings, Alpha is now making a major impact and providing the opportunity for churches of all denominations to adopt this significant model in obeying our Lord's command to "make disciples from every nation". I warmly commend the whole Alpha initiative.'

Clive Calver
President, World Relief

'The Alpha course is to me another example of the ongoing need for each successive generation to express its faith in contemporary terms and on current issues. I am not surprised to hear of its immediate acceptance and use by hundreds of churches all over the world and, furthermore, of the consequent decisions for Christ that it has generated. More power to Jesus!'

The late John Wimber
Association of Vineyard Churches

'One of the most effective tools of evangelism in the body of Christ in the United Kingdom is the Alpha course. This new and effective course has exploded, being used by hundreds of churches resulting in thousands of new believers being integrated into the local church. The enthusiasm is spreading rapidly. I wholeheartedly recommend Nicky Gumbel's excellent leadership. God has blessed the church greatly in raising up Nicky to trumpet the Alpha course.'

Mike Bickle
Metro Vineyard Fellowship, Kansas City

'God has used the Alpha ministry in a significant way to reach the seeking pre-Christians of England. We, in an increasingly secularised North

America, have much we can learn from the Alpha leaders about the principles which have enabled them to reach a biblically illiterate generation. I warmly commend the leaders of these conferences and the information they will present.'

Leighton Ford
Leighton Ford Ministries

'I see Alpha as a strategic tool, sensitively crafted to address today's secularised seekers with satisfying answers to their spiritual hunger. I recommend Alpha to all pastors wanting to equip their people for new-millennium effectiveness in evangelism.'

Jack W. Hayford
Pastor, The Church on the Way
President, The King's Seminary

'Alpha builds churches. By taking spiritual seekers step-by-step through their unanswered questions, Alpha builds strong believers and renewed passion. That is why Alpha is such a huge success.'

Bob Buford
Founder of Leadership Network

'Alpha courses are proving incredibly successful as an evangelistic format to reach people with the relevance of the gospel for our generation. The UK is being widely impacted by them and I would wholeheartedly encourage Christians in the USA to open their doors to the full impact of the ministry of Alpha.'

Terry Virgo
New Frontiers International

'I have met many unlikely people from different backgrounds who have been profoundly changed through attending this course.'

Jackie Pullinger
Hong Kong

'Alpha is an excellent introductory course for those who do not go to church or for whom an inherited Christianity has little meaning. I have no hesitation in recommending it to any church or group wishing to present the basic gospel message clearly and effectively.'

Charles Whitehead
International Catholic Charismatic Services

'The Alpha course is a superbly produced tool which, if used prayerfully and systematically, could be revolutionary . . . The relaxed, non-threatening but crystal-clear presentations of the talks could not fail to impact decisively both believer and enquirer alike. I am sold on Alpha and so is African Enterprise. We'll be using it and we hope you will too.'

Michael Cassidy
African Enterprise

'I am very impressed with the Alpha programme and with the evangelistic breakthroughs that you get with Alpha courses.'

Moss Ntlah
Concerned Evangelicals, South Africa

'Alpha seems especially blessed in that the Lord is using it to reach all sorts of people in all sorts of spiritual conditions.'

Luis Palau
Evangelist

'Alpha – not just the first letter of the Greek alphabet, but first choice for an illuminating perspective on Christianity. An ideal follow-up course for missions.'

J. John
Evangelist

'One of the most significant developments in evangelism in recent years and one of the most valuable resources for the church to emerge in the course of the Decade of Evangelism. Alpha is a proven, thoroughly tested, well researched, marvellously presented way of communicating the gospel in today's culture. It is being used to reach thousands of people with the heart of the Christian message.'

Canon Robert Warren
National Officer for Evangelism

'Alpha courses have been successfully used among our Pioneer network of churches. They are an increasing resource to those wanting to see people find forgiveness and favour in God's eyes. The course is fun and unthreatening – just like our Lord himself!'

Gerald Coates
Director, Pioneer

'The Alpha course for the enquirer into the Christian faith, as well as for new Christians, is one of the most exciting, successful, and God-owned and blessed courses in our current decade. I recommend it without any reservations – we've seen it working in our own fellowship with great inspiration.'

Roger Forster
Ichthus Christian Fellowship

'Alpha has proved its worth as a means of communicating the Christian faith in our contemporary culture.'

Elizabeth Caswell
Moderator, The United Reformed Church

'Alpha is easily the best Christian foundation course I know of. We found it exciting, easy to grasp and practical – *excellent!* I heartily endorse it.'

Paul Mercy
Former Assistant General Superintendent, Assemblies of God

'Alpha brings together so many aspects of what God is doing today; it is a tool of our time.'

Ken Gott
Sunderland Christian Centre (Assemblies of God)

'Alpha is a soul winning, discipling, multiplying, spiritually dynamic ministry that has already touched the lives of thousands. I believe this vision will continue to expand and truly become an international blessing.'

Loren Cunningham
Youth With A Mission International

'Alpha, as developed by Nicky Gumbel and the leaders of HTB, employs all the best principles for effective evangelism – that is why it is so fruitful.'

Lynn Green
Director of Europe, Middle East and Africa Department, YWAM

'The Alpha courses are being used extensively in this diocese and are proving to be an effective means of evangelism here in both urban and suburban areas. The user-friendly style is transforming many congregations and their approach to outreach.'

Michael Dickens Whinney
Assistant Bishop, Diocese of Birmingham

'Nicky Gumbel loves Christ, is a student of the Word and has a passion for the things that Christ had on his heart . . . the lost and his people.'

Paul Stanley
Vice President, The Navigators

'The great command to make disciples of all people is still relevant. Alpha provides us with contemporary cringe-free evangelism which deserves the increasing profile it is currently receiving.'

Joel Edwards
General Director, Evangelical Alliance UK

'In our task of sharing the gospel as it is, with people where they are, Alpha is a creative and contemporary means of successfully doing this. I love it and think it is inspired!'

Lyndon Bowring
Executive Chairman of CARE

'One of the most significant evangelistic enterprises since Billy Graham in the 1950s.'

David Pytches
Former Vicar of St Andrew's, Chorleywood

'Alpha is the most effective and transferable introductory course to the Christian faith that I know.'

Steve Chalke
Oasis Trust

'I commend the Alpha courses because I know that many hundreds of our Baptist churches have found them very helpful – for introducing rank outsiders to the local church and reaching fringe members of the church and drawing them into the mainstream.'

John C. James
President, Baptist Union of Great Britain, 1996–7

'Alpha has proved a ready and valuable tool for the churches in the Eastern area as they have sought to engage in relevant and sensitive evangelism.'

Paul Hills
General Superintendent, The Baptist Union of Great Britain

'Alpha has been used to bring many to a personal, living faith. What I find significant is how it cuts across boundaries to reach people who have little or no contact with the church. It continues to be a tool God uses.'

Ian Coffey
Vice Chair, Spring Harvest

'The Alpha course has been of enormous value to churches in strengthening fellowship and increasing effective evangelism in the local community.'

David Coffey
General Secretary, Baptist Union

'Alpha . . . is based on the local church, sees evangelism as a process which involves the whole of a person, and has much to say about the power and work of the Holy Spirit in the church's evangelistic outreach. I am happy to commend it, and trust that many individuals and churches will find increasing help with the Alpha courses.'

The late Revd Dr Donald English
Former General Secretary, Methodist Home Mission Division

'I firmly believe Alpha is a gift of God to the church in this day and give thanks for its continued success in bringing people into a relationship with Jesus. As part of the national evangelism team in the Methodist

Church, I will be offering Alpha as a key tool within any church mission programme.'

Ashley Cooper
Methodist Evangelism Enabler Co-ordinator

'Alpha is the most effective means of evangelism using small groups that I know. John Wesley's class meeting rediscovered.'

Rob Frost
National Evangelist, Methodist Church

'There is nothing like Alpha! Our prayer is that it will be discovered by many other churches throughout the world.'

John and Christine Noble
Pioneer

'The Alpha course is one of the most exciting evangelistic initiatives that has come to the church in the last decade. Don't miss it!'

Rob Parsons
Executive Director, Care for the Family

'I am quite certain that Alpha is crucial to evangelism in this country: it is Bible-centred, adaptable across traditions and denominations and above all answers the two most important yearnings that Springboard has found as it has gone around the UK – for basic teaching in the gospel and for a deeper spirituality.

It is tremendously adaptable and I know of its uses in Roman and Anglo-Catholic churches, as well as in Pentecostal and Baptist churches. It is also adaptable in terms of numbers. Springboard's experience is that Alpha is at the cutting edge of evangelism in this country at the moment.'

Martin Cavender
Administrative Director of Springboard, an initiative of the
Archbishops of Canterbury and York for the Decade of Evangelism

'Alpha is the most effective evangelistic tool for churches today. I hope every church will consider using it.'

Stephen Macchia
President of Vision New England

How to Run the Alpha Course

Nicky Gumbel

Alpha

First published 1994 as *Telling Others*
Revised 1997
Revised 2001
Revised 2004
New edition 2007
Revised 2010

ISBN: 978 1 905887 76 7

Text illustrations by Charlie Mackesy.

Scripture quotations taken from the HOLY BIBLE NEW INTERNATIONAL
VERSION © 1973, 1978, 1984 by International Bible Society.
Used by permission of Hodder & Stoughton Publishers, A member of the
Hachette Livre UK Group.
All rights reserved.
"NIV" is a registered trademark of International Bible Society.
UK trademark number 1448790.

Published by Alpha International
Holy Trinity Brompton
Brompton Road
London SW7 1JA
Email: publications@alpha.org

Contents

Foreword

As we look around at the state of the church, the figures of declining congregations, the crumbling buildings, the general sense of failure that haunts so much of the body of Jesus Christ today, there is a temptation for many of us involved in Christian ministry to feel discouraged. St Paul faced the same situation, yet he was able to say, 'Therefore, since through God's mercy we have this ministry, we do not lose heart' (2 Corinthians 4:1).

It isn't that people are not interested in spirituality – interest in the occult, religious experiences, spiritism, and other related forms of alternative searches is as great today as ever it was – but the universal spiritual hunger, that need to fill the God-shaped hole, has not been met by those things. The experience of those at Holy Trinity Brompton has been that people are now showing a new interest in the claims of Jesus Christ and the Christian faith. As our society moves into a post-Christian era many who are ignorant of the basic claimed truth of Christianity are wanting to find out more about Jesus of Nazareth, especially if they can be sure of an atmosphere of acceptance, without feeling threatened, judged or made to look foolish. I think that is one of the reasons why the Alpha course has proved to be such a success. The issues are clearly put and the claims of Christ examined, all in the company of other searchers and in an atmosphere of love and acceptance.

Nicky Gumbel inherited Alpha over fifteen years ago and, since then, by taking account of literally thousands of questionnaires, has adapted and improved the course so it is truly moulded to the perceived and experienced needs of those who attend. Without taking anything for granted, stripping the gospel down to its bare essentials, he has made Christianity accessible to this generation.

But it is not simply hard work which has brought about the growth of Alpha. The touch of the Holy Spirit has brought the course to life from beginning to end. Hunger is created, in the hearts of those who are taking part, for the reality of God. The Spirit alone can satisfy them. By revealing the reality of the power of Jesus Christ to forgive, to release, empower and equip, new life begins for so many who are in need of God.

At the time of going to print, there are currently thousands of Alpha courses running throughout this country and in other parts of the world. They range from small groups of five people to larger courses like one that is running at Holy Trinity at the moment, with over 700 people attending.

I know that you will enjoy this book. I am confident too that by God's grace you will find many people coming into the kingdom as a result of putting into practice the principles here.

Sandy Millar
Former Vicar of Holy Trinity Brompton

Preface

Thousands of people around the world are now taking part in Alpha courses – a ten week practical introduction to the Christian faith, designed primarily for non-churchgoers and those who have recently become Christians. In May 1993 we hosted a conference at Holy Trinity Brompton for church leaders who wanted to run such courses. Over a thousand people came, and hundreds of Alpha courses began all over the UK as a result. Since then we have held a number of regional conferences and have also been invited to do some international conferences. The number of Alpha courses in operation is growing daily. Having surveyed thousands of churches who are running Alpha, we have discovered that those who have attended an Alpha conference (tend to) experience a far greater degree of success on their courses. In the light of this, we strongly recommend that churches bring a leadership team to one of the numerous conferences that are held throughout the world. A list of these can be obtained from Holy Trinity Brompton.

This book is intended primarily to be a resource for churches who wish to run an Alpha course, although many of the principles of evangelism will have a wider application.

Alpha has evolved from what was essentially a basic introduction for new Christians to something which is aimed primarily at those outside the church. It was started at Holy Trinity Brompton in 1977 by Anglican clergyman Charles Marnham as a four-week course for new Christians. John Irvine took it over in 1981; he lengthened it to ten weeks and added a weekend for teaching on the person and work of the Holy Spirit. When Nicky Lee took it over in 1985 there were about thirty-five people on each course and under his leadership that grew to well over a hundred. Since then it has grown again to over 700 people (including the leadership team) on each course (three a year). It seems sensible to pass on some of the things we have learned over the years.

In addition to the theological principles and the practical details of how courses are run, each alternate chapter consists of a testimony of someone whose life has been changed by God through an Alpha course. Each person writes in their own individual style, having recorded their experiences while the events were still fresh in their memory. Nigel Skelsey's story is taken from a letter he wrote days after his conversion to Christ. The others are based on interviews given to Mark Elsdon-Dew and originally published in *Focus* newspaper of which he is the editor. He has kindly allowed me to include this material in the book.

Most of my experience of the course has been with the evening Alpha course at Holy Trinity Brompton; in Appendix C I have included an account by Deirdre Hurst on her experience of running a daytime Alpha.

I would like to express my thanks to Jon Soper, who has acted as a researcher for this and all the other Alpha resource books. I am so grateful for his thoroughness, speed and efficiency as well as his very perceptive comments and suggestions.

I am grateful to all the people who have read the manuscripts and offered their valuable insights and criticisms. I want to thank especially Jo Glen, Patricia Hall, Helena Hird, Simon Levell, Ken Costa, Tamsen Carter, the Revd Alex Welby, Judy Cahusac, Nicola Hinson, Chris Russell and Simon Downham.

Finally, a big thank you to Philippa Pearson Miles for her appendix on Administration and for typing the manuscript and organising the project with her extraordinary combination of speed and enthusiasm, together with calmness and patience.

Nicky Gumbel

1

Principles

I am not a natural evangelist. I have never found it easy to tell others about Jesus Christ. Some people are completely natural evangelists; they find it the easiest thing in the world. I recently heard about one man who seizes every opportunity to talk to people about Jesus. If he is standing at a bus stop and the bus is late, he turns that situation into a conversation about the Second Coming! I have another friend who is a tremendously confident evangelist and speaks about Jesus wherever he goes. On a train he will speak to the person opposite about Jesus. If he's walking along the street he will turn to someone and get into conversation with them about Jesus. On one occasion when he and his family went to a Happy Eater, he banged the table and called for silence in the restaurant. He then stood up and preached the gospel for five minutes. He says that at the end people came up to him and said, 'Thank you very much, that was very helpful.' I could not do that.

I first became a Christian over thirty years ago. I was so excited about what had happened that I longed for everybody to follow suit. After I had been a Christian for only a few days I went to a party, determined to tell everyone. I saw a friend dancing and decided the first step was to make her realise her need. So I went up to her and said, 'You look awful. You really need Jesus.' She thought I had gone mad. It was not the most effective way of telling someone the good news. (However, she did later become a Christian, quite independently of me, and she is now my wife!)

If we charge around like a bull in a china shop, sooner or later we will get hurt. Even if we approach the subject sensitively, we may still get hurt. When we do, we tend to withdraw. Certainly this was my experience. After a few years, I moved from the danger of insensitivity and fell into the opposite danger of fear. There was a time (ironically when I was at theological college) when I became fearful of even talking about Jesus to those who were not Christians. On one occasion, a group of us went from college to a parish mission on the outskirts of Liverpool, to tell people the good news. Each night we had supper with different people from the parish. One night a friend of mine called Rupert and I were sent to a couple who were on the fringe of the church (or to be more accurate, the wife was on the fringe and the husband was not a churchgoer). Halfway through the main course the husband asked me what we were doing up there. I stumbled, stammered, hesitated and prevaricated. He kept repeating the question. Eventually Rupert said straight out, 'We have come here to tell people about Jesus.' I felt deeply embarrassed and hoped the ground would swallow us all up! I realised how frozen with fear I had become and that I was afraid even to take the name of Jesus on my lips.

Ever since then I've been looking for ways in which ordinary people like me, who aren't naturally gifted evangelists, can communicate their faith with friends, family and colleagues without feeling fearful or risking insensitivity. That is why I was so excited to discover Alpha. One simple definition of Alpha is that it is 'evangelism for ordinary people'.

During the 1990s the number of people attending church on an average Sunday in Britain dropped by one million, according to a survey carried out by Christian Research. By 2002, figures from the Church of England's electoral rolls showed that membership had fallen by twelve per cent in a single year.[1] Despite this overall decrease, attendance among children and young people under sixteen increased by one per cent during the same period.[2] The vast majority of the population of the United Kingdom do not attend church, and of those who do, many only go at Christmas or Easter. Following in the wake of the decline in Christian belief, there has been a decline in the moral climate. The fabric of our society is unravelling. Every day in Britain at least 440 couples are divorced, 150 babies are born to teenage mothers and 480 babies are aborted. In addition, at least one new crime is committed every six seconds and a violent attack takes place every nine minutes. Although there were 30,000 Christian clergy of all types, there were more than 80,000 registered witches and fortune tellers.[3]

But at the same time, shoots of new life are springing up all over the place. New churches are being planted and many churches are seeing growth, sometimes slow and sometimes quite dramatic. Many Christian initiatives that arose out of the renewal movement in the Decade of Evangelism continue to build and encourage the church. One of those new shoots is the Alpha course. All of us involved with it have sensed the extraordinary blessing of God upon it.

I realise that we need to be cautious about saying this is a work of God. I know the story of the man who came up to a preacher and said, 'That was a great talk.' The preacher rather piously replied, 'It wasn't me, it was the Lord,' to which the man responded, 'It wasn't that good!' In saying that we believe Alpha is a work of God I am not for a moment suggesting that it is perfect. I'm sure that it is greatly marred by human error and frailty. There is much room for improvement and we try to listen carefully to constructive criticism. Nor do we believe that it is the only method of evangelism that God is blessing: far from it. Nevertheless, all the signs point to it being an extraordinary work of God and we are deeply grateful.

When Alpha first started growing I thought, 'How could something that started in Central London work elsewhere?' Alpha currently runs in more than 158 countries: in Zimbabwe, Kenya, Norway, Denmark, Sweden, Germany, Malaysia, Hong Kong, Australia, New Zealand, Japan, India, Korea, the United States, Canada and many others.

While at an Alpha conference in Zimbabwe, I discovered that Alpha was not only running among the English-speaking white Zimbabweans but also among the Shona-speaking people in their own language. Zimbabwe has a population of just over 10 million people: there are 90,000 whites in Zimbabwe but 90 per cent of the black population speak Shona. While I was at the conference I met a man called Edward Ngamuda. He had originally done Alpha in English but then thought that he would like to run the course in Shona. A couple who have come to Christ on Alpha owned a farm with 900 workers. They asked him to come and run the course for those who worked on their farm. Thirty people came on the first course and fifty came on the second. I asked him whether these people were Christians when they came on the course. 'No,' he replied, 'we had a Muslim, a witchdoctor and a polygamist come.' I asked how the polygamist happened to be there and was told that his first wife came on the first course, and that she had brought him and the other two wives on the next one! Edward assured me that Alpha worked better in Shona than it did in English. It was then that I began to realise that this course, which started in London, could operate in different countries and cultures. Why is this?

I believe it is because Alpha is based on six New Testament principles; in this first chapter, I want to look at each of these principles in turn.

Evangelism[4] is most effective through the local church

John Stott, author of many books and Rector Emeritus of All Souls, Langham Place, has described evangelism through the local church as 'the most normal, natural and productive method of spreading the gospel today'.[5] Similarly, in March 1998 at the US Bishops' Ad Limina address, Pope John II affirmed that the parish will necessarily be the centre of the new evangelisation. There are at least four reasons for this.

What you see is what you get

Missions and Billy Graham-style crusades clearly have been greatly used by God. They raise the profile of the church and are still an effective means of bringing people to Christ. In our church we often take teams on missions to universities and elsewhere and we appreciate the value and fruitfulness of this type of evangelism. But missions are more likely to bear lasting fruit if they are earthed in an ongoing programme of local church evangelism, because they then have the great advantage of continuity of relationships. Someone may respond at a crusade or mission and be referred to their local church. They may be disappointed to find the environment of the church radically different from the meeting which attracted them in the first place and so they subsequently stop attending. This is one of the reasons why the follow-up after big crusades is so hard. By contrast, if someone is introduced to Christianity at their local church, they become familiar with the place and the people, and are therefore much more likely to stay. We are finding on Alpha that belonging comes before believing for many people.

It mobilises a whole army of evangelists

In every church there are people who have gifts which can be used in evangelism but often their gifts are not recognised. For example, a Gallup survey discovered that only 10 per cent of American church members are active in any kind of personal ministry. However, an additional 40 per cent expressed an interest in having a ministry, but did not know how to start. This group is an untapped gold mine.

On every Alpha course, approximately one third of the people involved are hosts and helpers, all of them doing evangelism. Tens of thousands of people are now involved. Steve Morgan, the Rural Dean of Merthyr Tydfil in South Wales, put it like this:

It has been the heart cry of past generations to put evangelism within the grasp of ordinary people who are terrified at the thought of evangelism. This has never happened before. We have here 'a history-making-thing'. For generations, the only people who would touch evangelism were those with an outgoing personality. But now the shy little old lady can embrace evangelism for the first time. It has never been available for all types of personality before. Any church, at any time, with any group can run with this. We believe that the nation has been praying, and calling out for this, for generations.

It is friendship based

Alpha is a New Testament model of evangelism: Peter brought his brother Andrew; Philip brought his friend Nathaniel; the woman at the well went back and told everyone in her town; and Matthew the tax collector threw a party and invited all his work colleagues to meet Jesus. Pope Paul VI said, 'It is unthinkable that a person should accept the word and give himself to the kingdom without becoming a person who bears witness to it and proclaims it in his turn.'[6]

The pattern on Alpha is that people come to Christ and are filled with the Spirit. They then realise the wonder, the importance, and the relevance of what God has done for them through Christ and they want to tell their friends, family and work colleagues. Most of these others probably do not go to church nor are they Christians. Some of these in turn come and do the course. Some of them come to Christ, and are filled with the Spirit. They too become excited about Jesus and tell *their* friends, family and colleagues. In this way we find that we are constantly breaking into new circles of unchurched people.

The more checkouts, the more customers

One crusade may bring great blessing but it is limited both in time and space. If every local church in the world was running an effective ongoing programme of local church evangelism and every month people were coming to Christ and bringing their friends and these friends then brought other friends – imagine how quickly the world would be reached for Christ!

Michael Green, Advisor in Evangelism to the Archbishops of Canterbury and York, in his book *Evangelism through the Local Church*, summed up the need for this kind of evangelism:

> Whenever Christianity has been at its most healthy, evangelism has stemmed from the local church, and has had a noticeable impact on the surrounding area. I do not believe that the re-Christianisation of the West can take place without the renewal of local churches in this whole area of evangelism. We need a thoughtful, sustained, relevant presentation of the Christian faith, in word and in action, embodied in a warm, prayerful, lively local church which has a real concern for its community at all levels. . . . Such evangelism, in and from the local church, is not only much needed but . . . eminently possible. I believe it to be the most natural, long-lasting and effective evangelism that is open to us. If local churches were engaging in loving, outgoing evangelism within their neighbourhoods, many of our evangelistic campaigns, missions and crusades would be rendered much less necessary.[7]

EVANGELISM IS A PROCESS

Conversion may take place in a moment but it is part of a process. Jesus used the expression 'born again' (John 3:3) for the beginning of a spiritual life, and the New Testament speaks about becoming a child of God. While the birth of a child may be one event, there is a much longer process before and afterwards. The Bible uses many other images to represent spiritual growth: some are taken from agriculture, others from the ideas of building or journeying. All these involve a process. That is why, in many ways, I prefer the word 'evangelisation' used mainly by Roman Catholics, as it seems to reflect the New Testament understanding of conversion as the start of the Christian life.

Alpha is a ten-week course involving a total of fifteen talks which include a weekend and a celebration party at the end. We do not expect people to respond to the gospel after the first week (although some do). We recognise that people need time to think, watch, listen, and to talk through their questions and difficulties. Each person is beginning at a different stage.

Some are already Christians but will often say, in retrospect, that at the start of the course they were Christians 'without any real experience of God'. Others are at the point of new birth when they begin Alpha. Some have already given their lives to Christ at the party at the end of the previous course, others at a guest service before the beginning of Alpha. Still others perhaps come to faith through the witness of their family or a friend. Many are still a long way off when they begin Alpha. Some are convinced atheists, some are New Agers, some are adherents to other religions or cults. Many are living in lifestyles which are far from Christian. Some are alcoholics, others are compulsive gamblers, many are living with partners they are not married to and some are in a homosexual lifestyle. We welcome them all. Some will complete the whole course and still not be Christians at the end; we hope they will be unable to say they have not heard the gospel. Others will give their lives to Christ somewhere on the course. For nearly all of them, Alpha will enable them to take a step forward in their relationship with God.

The fact that there is a process spread over fifteen sessions enables us to give longer to aspects of the Christian faith than one would be able to in one evangelistic talk. For example, in 1994 I saw a man standing at the back of the room who looked very suspicious and worried. When I introduced myself he said, 'I don't want to be here, I've been dragged along.' I said, 'Great! Let me introduce you to eleven other people who don't want to be here,' and I took him to meet my small group. At the end of the evening I heard him chatting to someone else in the group.

'Are you coming back next week?'

The other man replied, 'Yes, I'll be here.'

To which the first man said, 'Well, if you're coming back next week, I'll come back next week.'

Six weeks later he said to me, 'This course is like a jigsaw puzzle. Every time I come back another piece fits into place. And I'm beginning to get the picture.'

Furthermore, the fact that Alpha is a process enables trust to develop. There is a great deal of cynicism, scepticism and distrust about the Christian church. I had no idea of the extent of this until I spoke to someone who said that for the first three weeks of the course he had not eaten the food in case it was drugged. That was an extreme case of distrust but many people wonder if the church is after their money, their mind or something else. It can take a few weeks for a level of trust to build. As the guests get to know their small group hosts, they begin to see that they are not 'after' anything and they start to listen.

EVANGELISM INVOLVES THE WHOLE PERSON

Evangelism involves an appeal to the whole person. Pope John Paul II, speaking to bishops from Japan, said that 'evangelisation . . . must touch people's minds and hearts, stir their consciences and engage all their energies'. Indeed, each talk on Alpha is designed to appeal to the mind, heart, conscience and will, although in some of the talks the emphasis will be on just one of those aspects.

We appeal to the mind because we believe that Christianity is based in history: on the life, death and resurrection of Jesus Christ. We preach 'Jesus Christ and him crucified' (1 Corinthians 2:2). We seek to persuade with every argument we can muster, just as Paul did on so many occasions (eg Acts 18:4). We try to teach only what we can establish from the Bible and we point people to the biblical text. We do not expect anyone to take a 'blind leap' of faith. Rather, we hope they will take a step of faith based on reasonable grounds.

Secondly, we appeal to the heart. Our message does not simply require an assent of the intellect to a series of propositions; rather it calls people to a love-relationship with Jesus Christ. John Stott has written:

> There is a place for emotion in spiritual experience. The Holy Spirit's . . . ministry is not limited to illuminating our minds and teaching us about Christ. He also pours God's love into our hearts. Similarly, he bears witness with our spirit that we are God's children, for he causes us to say 'Abba, father' and to exclaim with gratitude, 'How great is the love the father has lavished on us, that we should be called children of God!' . . . I think it was Bishop Handley Moule at the end of the last century who gave this good advice: 'Beware equally of an undevotional theology (ie mind without heart) and of an untheological devotion (ie heart without mind).'[8]

Graham Cray, Bishop of Maidstone and principal of Ridley Hall theological college in Cambridge, has spoken with great insight about the contemporary culture which is in the process of shifting from an Enlightenment culture to a new and coming one. In the Enlightenment, reason reigned supreme and explanation led to experience. In the present transitional culture with its 'pick-and-mix' worldview, in which the New Age movement is a potent strand, experiences lead to explanation.

The Pope, speaking to young people in Italy, asked them this: 'If your faith is not based on experience, how can you account for your hope to yourselves and others? How can you overcome the doubts and crises that are so characteristic of your age? Open the doors of your hearts to the experience of the Lord.' I have often found that many older people approach Alpha from an essentially Enlightenment perspective. They feel at home with the parts of the course which appeal to the mind, but often have difficulty in experiencing the Holy Spirit. Others, often the younger guests, coming from the New Age movement find that rational and historical explanations leave them cold, but at the weekend away they are on more familiar territory in experiencing the Spirit. Previously they will have been seeking experiences which have then left them discontented and only in experiencing a relationship with God through Jesus Christ do they find their hunger is satisfied.

The gospel involves both the rational and the experiential and it impacts both those from an Enlightenment background who need to experience God and those who have sought experiences but who need to understand the truth about God.

Thirdly, we seek to appeal to the conscience. Paul writes, 'By setting forth the truth plainly we commend ourselves to everyone's conscience in the sight of God' (2 Corinthians 4:2). We know that every person has a conscience. Deep down we all have a sense of right and wrong. The Holy Spirit, often working through people's conscience, convinces them about sin. Their consciences therefore are on our side. Throughout the course we are appealing to this side in urging people to repent and turn to Christ.

Fourthly, we seek to appeal to the will. We recognise, of course, that no one can come to the Father unless God calls them. As Jesus said, 'No-one knows the Son except the Father, and no-one knows the Father except the Son and those to whom the Son chooses to reveal him' (Matthew 11:27). On the other hand, Jesus went on to say in the very next verse, 'Come to me, all you who are weary and burdened, and I will give you rest' (Matthew 11:28). In other words, he called for a decision.

There is a difference between an appeal to the will and the

wrong form of pressure. We try to avoid all forms of pressure on Alpha. We do not endlessly exhort anyone to respond, or chase people up if they do not come back: it is up to them to decide. Over the period of ten weeks, as we pray and allow the Holy Spirit to do his work, giving people the opportunity to respond, we are, in effect, making a continuous appeal to their wills.

MODELS OF EVANGELISM IN THE NEW TESTAMENT INCLUDE CLASSICAL, HOLISTIC AND POWER EVANGELISM

Graham Tomlin, vice-principal at Wycliffe Hall theological college, Oxford, draws attention to three different models of evangelism. [9] Clearly these three are not mutually exclusive and we very much hope that the Alpha course involves all three models.

Classical evangelism – words

First, there is *classical evangelism* which involves 'the proclamation of the unchanging message'. Certainly, at the heart of Alpha is the proclamation of the gospel of Jesus Christ: the first talk is about Christ's deity, the second is about his death on the cross for us and each talk has at its core some principle of Christian belief and living.

We do not believe we have the liberty to tamper with the apostolic message. However, the message comes to us in a cultural packaging. Every generation has a duty to ensure that the packaging is not a stumbling block; to preserve the unchanging message but to change the packaging in order to make it understandable in the context of their own culture. Martin Luther translated the Scriptures into the German vernacular, and the Lutheran church adapted the folk music of the day into songs of worship. The Methodist church under the leadership of the Wesley brothers were 'agreed to become more vile to reach the common people and to speak in the most obvious, easy, common words, wherever our meaning can be conveyed'. General William Booth, the founder of the Salvation Army, memorably said, 'Why should the devil have all the good tunes?'

Pope John Paul II put it like this: 'The new evangelisation demands that you present with new methods the eternal and unchanging context of the heritage of our Christian faith.' In a similar vein Pope Paul VI wrote:

> On us particularly, the pastors of the church, rests the responsibility of re-shaping with boldness and wisdom, but in complete fidelity to the content of evangelisation, the means that are most suitable and effective for communicating the gospel message to the men and women of our times. . . The individual churches . . . have the task of assimilating the essence of the gospel message and of transposing it, without the slightest betrayal of its essential truth, into the language that those particular people understand, and then of proclaiming it in their language.

Holistic evangelism – works

Secondly, there is *holistic evangelism*. As John Stott wrote, 'We are convinced that God has given us social as well as evangelistic responsibilities in his world.'[10]

Evangelism and social action go hand in hand. The latter involves both social justice in the removal of injustice, inhumanity and inequality, and social service in relieving human need, such as hunger, homelessness and poverty. We attempt on Alpha to avoid the dangers of pietism by our teaching and example, believing that evangelism is fundamentally linked to social responsibility (see Appendix J).

As the late Bishop Lesslie Newbigin put it:

> Christian programmes for justice and compassion . . . severed from their proper roots in the liturgical and sacramental life of the congregation . . . lose their character as signs of the presence of Christ and risk becoming mere crusades fuelled by a moralism that can become self-righteous. And the life of the worshipping congregation, severed from its proper expression in compassionate service to the secular community around it, risks becoming a self-centred existence serving only the needs and desires of its members.[11]

Power evangelism – wonders

Thirdly, there is *power evangelism*, where the proclamation of the gospel goes hand in hand with a demonstration of the Spirit's power (1 Corinthians 2:1–5). We include this third element because we believe it is firmly based in New Testament practice.

It used to be argued that you cannot take doctrine from narrative, but New Testament scholars have shown to the satisfaction of theologians of all varieties that the gospel writers were not only historians, they were theologians as well. In a different literary form, they were writing theology as much as Paul or the other writers of the New Testament epistles. In the gospels, the central theme in the teaching of Jesus is the kingdom of God. The coming of the kingdom involved not only the spoken proclamation of the gospel but also a visible demonstration of its presence by signs, wonders and miracles. Each of the gospel writers expected these to continue.

We can see this from the way in which Matthew sets out his Gospel. He tells us that 'Jesus went throughout Galilee, teaching in their synagogues, preaching the good news of the kingdom, and healing every disease and sickness among the people' (Matthew 4:23). He then gives some of the teaching and preaching of Jesus in chapters 5–7 (the Sermon on the Mount), then nine miracles (mainly of healing) and he concludes with an almost exact repetition of Matthew 4:23: 'Jesus went through all the towns and villages, teaching in their synagogues, preaching the good news of the kingdom and healing every disease and sickness' (Matthew 9:35). Matthew is using a literary device of repetition known as an 'inclusio', a short piece of text which appears at the beginning and at the end of a particular section and which acts as punctuation by enclosing a theme. Having shown what Jesus himself did, Matthew tells us that Jesus then sent the Twelve out to do the same. He told them to go out and preach the same message: '"The kingdom of heaven is near." Heal the sick, raise the dead, cleanse those who have leprosy, drive out demons. . .' (Matthew 10:7–8).

At the end of his Gospel, Matthew makes it clear that Jesus expected all his disciples to 'go and make disciples of all nations . . . teaching them to obey *everything* I have commanded you' (Matthew 28:19–20, italics mine). This surely includes not only his ethical teaching, but also the earlier commissions.

In Mark's Gospel we see a similar pattern. Mark tells us that Jesus proclaimed the good news (Mark 1:14 onwards) demonstrating it by signs and wonders (Mark 1:21 onwards). The kingdom of God was inaugurated by Jesus and is still growing to this day. There is no reason why its fundamental nature should have changed. Indeed, in the longer ending of Mark (which is, at the very least, good evidence of what the early church believed Jesus' commission to be) Jesus said, '"Go into all the world and preach the good news to all creation . . . and these signs will accompany *those who believe*. In my name they will drive out demons . . . they will place their hands on sick people, and they will get well.. . ."' Then the disciples went out and preached everywhere, and the Lord worked with them and confirmed his word by the signs that accompanied it' (Mark 16:15–20, italics mine). Jesus says, 'These signs will accompany *those who believe*' – that is to say, those who believe in Jesus Christ, which means all Christians.

For Luke's theology we need to look at both Luke and Acts. Luke tells us in his Gospel: 'When Jesus had called the Twelve together, he gave them power and authority to drive out all demons and to cure diseases, and he sent them out to preach the kingdom of God and to heal the sick' (Luke 9:1–2). Nor was it only the Twelve to whom he gave this commission; he also appointed seventy-two others and told them to go out and 'heal the sick who are there and tell them, "The kingdom of God is near you"' (Luke 10:9).

In the book of Acts this continues beyond the time Jesus was on earth. After the outpouring of the Holy Spirit, there is a remarkable continuation of supernatural power, ranging from speaking in tongues to raising the dead. These demonstrations of power continue right through to the last chapter (Acts 28:7–9). In the Acts of the Apostles we see the outworking of this commission. The disciples continued to preach and teach, but also to heal the sick, raise the dead and cast out demons (Acts 3:1–10; 4:12; 5:12–16; 8:5–13; 9:32–43; 14:3, 8–10; 19:11–12; 20:9–12; 28:8–9).

Nor is this ministry in the Spirit's power confined to the synoptic gospels. In John's Gospel Jesus is recorded as saying, in the context of miracles, 'All who have faith in me will do what I have been doing, and they will do even greater things than these, because I am going to the Father' (John 14:12). Clearly no one has performed miracles of greater quality than Jesus, but there has been a greater quantity since Jesus returned to the Father. He has not ceased to perform miracles, but now he uses weak and imperfect human beings. Again it says, 'All who have faith in me': that is, all Christians. These commands and promises are not restricted anywhere to a special category of people.

Signs and miracles were a central part of Paul's proclamation of the gospel (Romans 15:19). It is also clear from 1 Corinthians 12–14 that Paul did not believe that such abilities were confined to the apostles and he expected the more obviously supernatural gifts of the Spirit to continue in an effective and healthy church. He speaks about 'gifts of healing', 'miraculous powers', 'prophecy', 'speaking in different kinds of tongues' and 'the interpretation of tongues'. He described these as being given to different members of the body of Christ and as being the work of the Spirit (1 Corinthians 12:7–11).

Nowhere in the New Testament does it say that these gifts will cease at the end of the apostolic age. On the contrary, Paul says that they will only cease when 'perfection comes' (1 Corinthians 13:10). Some have identified 'perfection' here with the formation of the canon of Scripture, saying that as we now have the Bible, we have no need of 'imperfect' spiritual gifts. However, the context for this verse clearly shows that Paul is identifying 'perfection' with the return of Jesus. The world is not yet perfect, neither do we see Jesus 'face to face' (v 12), nor do we 'know fully' (v 12) but we know only 'in part' (v 12). This 'perfection' will only occur when Jesus returns and then these gifts will no longer be necessary. Until that moment they are a vital part of the church's armoury. Indeed, this passage shows that Paul did not expect the gifts to cease until the return of Jesus.

Likewise, the writer to the Hebrews says that God testified to his message by 'signs, wonders and various miracles, and gifts of the Holy Spirit' (Hebrews 2:4). Nowhere in the Bible is the supernatural display of the power of the Holy Spirit confined to any particular period of history. On the contrary, such signs, wonders and miracles are part of the kingdom which was inaugurated by Jesus Christ and continues to this day. Hence we should expect today to see the supernatural display of the power of the Holy Spirit as part of his kingdom activity and as an authentication of the good news. However, we do not draw ultimate attention to the signs and wonders, but to the God of love who performs them.

Evangelism in the power of the Holy Spirit is both dynamic and effective

On the Day of Pentecost such was the power with which Peter preached that the people were 'cut to the heart' and 3,000 were converted (Acts 2:37–41). The remarkable events continued: 'Everyone was filled with awe, and many wonders and miraculous signs were done by the apostles. . . . And the Lord added to their number daily those who were being saved' (Acts 2:43–47).

Remarkable healings followed (eg Acts 3:1–10). People were astonished and came running to find out what had happened (3:11). Peter and John preached the gospel with great boldness:

'When they saw the courage of Peter and John and realised that they were unschooled, ordinary men, they were astonished and they took note that these men had been with Jesus. But since they could see the man who had been healed standing there with them, there was nothing they could say' (Acts 4:13–14). The authorities had no idea what to do because 'all the people were praising God for what had happened. For the man who was miraculously healed was over forty years old' (Acts 4:21–22).

The dynamic effect on the crowds continued:

> The apostles performed many miraculous signs and wonders among the people. And all the believers used to meet together in Solomon's Colonnade. No-one else dared join them, even though they were highly regarded by the people. Nevertheless, more and more men and women believed in the Lord and were added to their number. As a result, people brought the sick into the streets and laid them on beds and mats so that at least Peter's shadow might fall on some of them as he passed by. Crowds gathered also from the towns around Jerusalem, bringing their sick and those tormented by evil spirits, and all of them were healed (Acts 5:12–16).

People continued to be converted. 'So the word of God spread. The number of disciples in Jerusalem increased rapidly, and a large number of priests became obedient to the faith' (Acts 6:7). As we go on in the book of Acts the same pattern continues. When Paul and Barnabas went to Iconium, 'they spoke so effectively that a great number of Jews and Gentiles believed' (Acts 14:1). They spent a considerable time there 'speaking boldly for the Lord, who confirmed the message of his grace by enabling them to do miraculous signs and wonders' (Acts 14:3). In Lystra a crippled man was healed (Acts 14:8). In Derbe 'they preached the good news in that city and won a large number of disciples' (Acts 14:21).

Later on, Luke tells us what happened to twelve Ephesian men: 'When Paul placed his hands on them, the Holy Spirit came on them, and they spoke in tongues and prophesied' (Acts 19:6). Further, in Ephesus, 'God did extraordinary miracles through Paul, so that even handkerchiefs and aprons that had touched him were taken to the sick, and their illnesses were cured and the evil spirits left them' (Acts 19:11–12).

Far from dwindling away through the period covered by the book of Acts, this spiritual dynamic continued. Even in the last chapter we read of Paul praying for Publius's father: 'His father was sick in bed, suffering from fever and dysentery. Paul went in to see him and, after prayer, placed his hands on him and healed him. When this had happened, the rest of the sick on the island came and were cured' (Acts 28:8–9). All the way through we see the dynamic effect of the coming of the kingdom of God accompanied by conversions, miraculous signs, healings, visions, tongues, prophecy, raising the dead and casting out evil spirits. The same God is at work today among us. Evangelism can still be dynamic and effective.

EFFECTIVE EVANGELISM REQUIRES THE FILLING AND REFILLING OF THE SPIRIT

Jesus told his disciples, 'You will receive power when the Holy Spirit comes on you; and you will be my witnesses in Jerusalem, and in all Judea and Samaria, and to the ends of the earth' (Acts 1:8). On the Day of Pentecost the promise of Jesus was fulfilled and 'all of them were filled with the Holy Spirit and began to speak in other tongues as the Spirit enabled them' (Acts 2:4).

However, it did not end there. Later on we read of Peter being 'filled with the Spirit' again (Acts 4:8). Still later the disciples (including Peter) were filled again (Acts 4:31). The filling of the Holy Spirit is not a one-off experience. Paul urges the Christians of Ephesus 'to be filled with the Spirit' (Ephesians 5:18) and the emphasis is on continuing to be filled. Professor Wayne Grudem writes the most useful chapter I know of on this subject in his masterful *Systematic Theology*.[12]

As we look at the great evangelists of more recent history we see how many speak of such experiences. St Philip Neri living in sixteenth century Rome, at the age of 29, on the night before Pentecost 1544, experienced an extraordinary visitation from God's Spirit. As he was absorbed in prayer, he saw a ball of fire enter his mouth and travel down to his heart. The sensation of intense heat – that all consuming fire of God's love – was so great that he threw himself on the ground to cool himself, pleading, 'Oh, enough Lord, enough. I can't take any more.' Filled with compassion, he began to spend time on the streets of Rome, looking for opportunities to share the gospel and pray for the sick, many of whom were miraculously healed. St Philip brought the joy of the Lord to an entire city. He was a priest who, by following the Spirit's prompting, spawned a revival.

John Wesley (1703–1791), the founder of modern Methodism, wrote of an occurrence on New Year's Day 1739:

> At about three in the morning, as we were continuing in prayer, the power of God came mightily upon us. Many cried out in complete

joy. Others were knocked to the ground. As soon as we recovered a little from that awe and amazement at God's presence, we broke out in praise.

The result was that 'the Holy Spirit began to move among us with amazing power when we met in his name'. When anyone fell down under the preaching, they were prayed for until they were 'filled with the peace and joy of the Holy Spirit', which was frequently 'received in a moment'. Wesley's journal is full of such accounts. One Quaker, who objected to such goings on, 'went down as thunderstruck' and rose to cry aloud: 'Now I know you are a prophet of the Lord.'

Wesley concluded: 'Similar experiences continued to increase as I preached. It seemed prudent to preach and write on the work of the Holy Spirit.'[13] He preached regularly at Bristol's Newgate prison where the jailer, Abel Dagge, had been converted under Whitefield in 1737:

> One Thursday Wesley preached on the text 'He that believeth hath everlasting life' and at the end he prayed 'If this is thy truth, do not delay to confirm it by signs following'. Immediately 'the power of God fell among us. One, and another, and another, sank to the earth . . . dropping on all sides as thunderstruck'. One, Ann Davies, cried out. He went across and prayed over her and she began to praise God in joy.[14]

For thirty-five years George Whitefield (1714–1770) was the outstanding itinerant preacher in Britain and America and he changed the conventions of preaching, opening the way for mass evangelism. He wrote in his journal: 'Was filled with the Holy Ghost. Oh, that all who deny the promise of the Father, might thus receive it themselves! Oh, that all were partakers of my joy!'[15]

Charles Grandison Finney (1792–1875) was one of history's greatest evangelists, considered by many to be the forerunner of modern evangelism. Finney's experience of the Holy Spirit occurred later on the same day as his conversion:

> The Holy Spirit descended upon me in a manner that seemed to go through me, body and soul. I could feel the impression, like a wave of electricity, going through and through me. Indeed, it seemed to come in waves and waves of liquid love; for I could not express it in any other way. And yet it did not seem like water but rather the breath of God. I can recollect distinctly that it seemed to fan me, like immense wings: and it seemed to me, as these waves passed over me, that they literally moved my hair like a passing breeze. No words can express the wonderful love that was shed abroad in my heart. I wept aloud with joy and love; and I do not know but I should say, I literally bellowed out the unutterable gushings of my heart. These waves came over me, and over me, and over me, one after another, until I recollect I cried out, 'I shall die if these waves continue to pass over me.' I said, 'Lord, I cannot bear any more;' yet I had no fear of death.[16]

Perhaps the greatest evangelist of the nineteenth century was D. L. Moody (1837–1899). Early on in his ministry he was a successful superintendent of a Sunday school mission in Chicago. However, two old ladies in his congregation informed him after a service that they were praying for him because he lacked the power of the Spirit. Although he was annoyed at their suggestion, the more he pondered about it the more he knew they were right. He wrote later that 'there came a great hunger into my soul. I did not know what it was. I began to cry out as I never did before. I really felt that I did not want to live if I could not have this power for service. . . . I was crying all the time that God would fill me with His Holy Spirit.' About six months later, as he was walking down Wall Street in New York City, the Holy Spirit came upon him powerfully. He wrote later:

> Oh! What a day, I cannot describe it! I seldom refer to it, it is almost too sacred an experience to name . . . I can only say God revealed Himself to me, and I had such an experience of His love that I had to ask Him to stay His hand.

John Pollock, his biographer, adds that Moody needed never thirst again. 'The dead, dry days were gone. "I was all the time tugging and carrying water. But now I have a river that carries me."'[17]

Moody's successor at his Bible Institute was the great American evangelist of the early nineteen hundreds, R. A. Torrey (1856–1928). In his book *The Baptism with the Holy Spirit* he wrote:

> It was a great turning point in my ministry when, after much thought and study and meditation, I became satisfied that the baptism with the Holy Spirit was an experience for today and for me, and set myself to obtain it. Such blessing came to me personally that I began giving Bible readings on the subject, and I have continued to do so with increasing frequency as the years have passed. . . . It has been the author's unspeakable privilege to pray with many ministers and Christian workers for this great blessing, and after to learn from them or from others of the new power that had come into their service, none other than the power of the Holy Spirit.[18]

In his book *Why God Used D. L. Moody* Will H. Houghton wrote:

> Some of our readers may take exception to Dr Torrey's use of the term 'the baptism with the Holy Ghost.' Perhaps if Dr Torrey lived in our day and saw some of the wildfire in connection with that expression,

he would use some other phrase. But let no one quibble about an experience as important as the filling of the Spirit. In this little book Dr Torrey quotes Mr Moody as saying, in a discussion on this very matter, 'Oh, why will they split hairs? Why don't they see that this is just the one thing that they themselves need? They are good teachers, they are wonderful teachers, and I am so glad to have them here, but why will they not see that the baptism of the Holy Ghost is just the one touch that they themselves need?'

I think that there can be little doubt that the greatest evangelist of last century was Billy Graham (b. 1918). In his authorised biography John Pollock tells how Billy Graham visited Hildenborough Hall and heard Stephen Olford speak on the subject 'Be not drunk – but be filled with the Spirit'. Billy Graham asked to see Olford privately and Olford expounded the fullness of the Holy Spirit in the life of a believer. 'At the close of the second day they prayed, "like Jacob of old laying hold of God,"' recalls Olford, 'crying, "Lord, I will not let Thee go except Thou bless me", until we came to a place of rest and praising;' and Graham said, 'This is a turning-point in my life. This will revolutionise my ministry.'[19]

In 1977, Raniero Cantalamessa, preacher to the Papal Household and Franciscan Professor of Theology, prayed to be filled with the Spirit. He had a vision of the cross:

I was convinced at that moment that this renewal goes straight to the heart of the gospel, which is the cross of Jesus Christ! . . . Somebody said: 'You will experience a new joy in proclaiming my word' . . . I can tell you this prophecy has come true. I have experienced a new joy in proclaiming the word of God . . . the Scriptures came alive . . . The love of Scripture which results from the Holy Spirit is unbelievable . . . I realised that I had a new desire for prayer . . . When the Spirit comes, he says: 'Abba, Abba.' . . . One day as I was praying in my cell in the friary, I prayed for the first time in a manner vaguely like speaking in tongues; not exactly the same, but somewhat similar. For a moment there was a very deep-down communication – nothing verbal or visible – but I sensed that Jesus was passing in front of me.[20]

One of the keys to Alpha is having a team of Spirit-filled people using every gift they possess to lead others to Christ. 'Evangelisation will never be possible without the action of the Holy Spirit,' concluded Pope Paul VI. Those who come to Christ on the course know that a radical change has occurred in their lives because they have been filled with the Holy Spirit. This experience of God gives them the stimulus and power to invite their friends to the next Alpha.

In the rest of this book I want to look at the practical outworking of this vision and intersperse it with stories of some of those whose lives have been changed by attending an Alpha course.

The story of
Nigel Skelsey

2

Nigel Skelsey

Nigel Skelsey rose quickly to the position of picture editor of a national newspaper, but felt he had lost his soul in the process. He joined an Alpha course at Holy Trinity Brompton and subsequently wrote a letter about the effect it had had on his life. With his permission, the letter is reproduced here.

Dear Nicky,

I was going to start this letter by saying, 'Just a short note to tell you what the Alpha weekend meant to me', but I'm afraid it's turned into a long note. Please bear with me, but it's something I feel I need to get down on paper.

In 1979 my father died of stomach cancer and it was at that time that my Christian faith went on the back burner, and for the last fifteen years I haven't known why. It wasn't, as one might suppose, the question of suffering and a loving God. That wasn't a problem for me. I have subsequently found out it was far more deep-rooted than a moral dilemma.

For most of my life I have felt I've been a huge disappointment both to God and my parents. When I left school I spent three years at theological college training to be a church minister with a genuine desire to be an evangelist, but I failed academically, ending up with the double burden of not only being looked upon by my parents as a failure but also, I felt, by God as well.

I decided to pursue a career in photography, which was a hobby of my father's, with the hope of winning my parents' approval, and I joined a publishing company as a tea boy on a newly-launched photographic magazine. I had been there six months when my father got ill and eventually died. Just two weeks after his death the staff, on what was an ailing magazine, were sacked or left of their own volition. The tea boy was the only one left and was promptly made editor by default. It was success of sorts and something of which my father would have been incredibly proud. But he wasn't there to see it and I was devastated.

For the next fifteen years there followed a faithless and obsessive pursuit of success for its own sake. Every time I achieved something I would knock it on the head and start again from scratch. I was like a child with building bricks. I would build a tower and shout, 'Look, Dad!' before knocking it down and building another one to impress him with.

My career was like a roller-coaster. The ailing magazine, more by luck than judgement, given my inexperience, was turned round and within two years was the biggest selling monthly photographic magazine in the country. At the height of its success, and after only two years in the job, I left to join another magazine which was in a poor state. Within two years circulation was surging to the point of overtaking the first magazine. Once more success came quickly, but it wasn't enough and after another two years I put an end to that and decided to launch my own photographic magazine which, within no time at all, became renowned around the world, picking up publishing awards along the way.

Another two years had gone by and I still wasn't satisfied, so in 1987 I decided that I wanted to be picture editor of a national newspaper. I had no experience in that particular industry and to all bar the totally demented it did not enter the realms of possibility. Since I was fast joining the ranks of the totally demented I didn't see the problem and within three years, at the grand old age of thirty-seven, I became the picture editor of *The Sunday Telegraph*.

Just before Christmas 1993 I turned forty and, probably like many on reaching that age, decided to reflect on what I had achieved and possibly where the next challenge lay. Forgetting the spiritual side, which was non-existent anyway, I was very satisfied. I had everything I had ever wanted in life: a fulfilling, well-paid job, a beautiful wife, two great sons, and, at one point I'm embarrassed to say, a Porsche 911. But at what cost?

I discovered that my nickname at *The Telegraph* was 'The Beast'. Despite the affectionate undertones that many nicknames have, it told me something about myself that I didn't like. I also overheard someone else say that I was not truly happy unless I was at war with someone. They were right. In fact, if conflict didn't happen to come my way then I created it. Life had become a great battlefield.

Jesus said, 'Love your neighbour as yourself,' but my trouble was that deep down I hated myself and I hated my neighbour as myself. My motto was: 'Forget revenge, get your retaliation in first!' I was like some ageing prize fighter who doesn't know when to give up. Every single day of the last fifteen years has been a brawl, only, unlike a boxing match, the bell never came at the end of each round. Worst of all I looked in the bathroom mirror one morning and saw reflected back someone I just didn't know any more. Over the next few days the words of Jesus kept coming back to me, 'What good will it be for a man if he gains the whole world, yet forfeits his soul?', and I realised that I had done just that. In my own little world I literally had everything I ever wanted but I had lost my soul in the process.

Then on New Year's Day a friend whom I hadn't seen for years came round to dinner. What struck me was that he wasn't the person I used to know. Even though a Christian, my old friend was the most dreadful pessimist, whose character I despised; the new version sitting in front of me was full of vigour, optimism and genuine happiness. And he started to tell me about the great work that the Holy Spirit had done in his life. He went on to describe how he had felt a failure all his life and how his father had been hugely disappointed in him and, without warning, I burst into inconsolable floods of tears at the dinner table: something The Beast was not prone to doing!

He was describing what was locked away deep in my subconscious and, although I didn't realise it, had been dominating my life all these years. Unrattled, he stood up and prayed over me and I felt the most extraordinary tingling sensation flooding through me, flushing out all the deep-rooted unhappiness that had slowly festered beneath the surface over the years.

I had experienced something I didn't understand, but which had a profound effect on me. I woke up the next morning like a man obsessed with a new ambition. I sensed God loved me and that I wasn't a write-off in his eyes. I was still heavily chained at the bottom of a deep dark prison, only someone had banged a hole in the wall and a chink of light was spilling in, giving me a taste of the freedom that was there if only I could grasp hold of it.

In the summer I had been on holiday in Switzerland and had read an article in a magazine I found about the Alpha course at Holy Trinity Brompton. The one thing that had stuck in my mind was how the work of the Holy Spirit was described as of paramount importance. I knew in my heart I had to have his power in my life at any cost so I found out where the church was, enrolled on the course and focused on the weekend. I felt like a dying man waiting for a life-saving operation. Never mind the weeks of premed, I just had to get into the operating theatre.

The weekend I had been waiting for, like a child waiting for Christmas, finally arrived . . . and I didn't want to go! I didn't realise what a spiritual battle I was about to experience. I lay in bed at the conference centre on the Friday night and went through an onslaught the like of which I have never experienced before and I hope I never do again. Voices screamed in my head to get out, go home, I was making a fool of myself, God wouldn't do anything for me, I was beyond hope, I was a failure and so on. I tried to pray but I couldn't. I just lay there for what seemed like hours and got the biggest mauling of my life.

I woke up in the morning shattered. I looked at the order of play, saw that the third session (which I had identified as the main one) was at 4.30 pm and simply hung on like a marathon runner weaving his way up the final straight with nothing but the finishing tape as the focus of his attention.

I'll never forget that final session. I felt as though I was being torn in two. Halfway through I just couldn't stand it any more.

The prize was so near but we were getting there so slowly! I literally wanted to scream out, 'Do it now! Do it now! I can't hold out any longer.' I'm not exaggerating when I say I was in agony. Then God came, and oh, the relief.

Do you know, for the first time in my life I feel normal. It seems a strange thing to say but it keeps hitting me just how normal I feel! I also feel loved. I am accepted for who I am and I feel free. Terribly clichéd, isn't it? But I feel so free!

Yesterday I read some words of Paul in Philippians which express so deeply how I now feel about my 'achievements' of the last fifteen years: 'But whatever was to my profit I now consider loss for the sake of Christ. What is more, I consider everything a loss compared to the surpassing greatness of knowing Christ Jesus my Lord, for whose sake I have lost all things. I consider them rubbish, that I may gain Christ and be found in him. . . . But one thing I do: Forgetting what is behind and straining towards what is ahead, I press on towards the goal to win the prize for which God has called me heavenwards in Christ Jesus' (Philippians 3:7–9, 13).

I don't know what the future holds or where and how God will lead me; at the moment I'm just enjoying a honeymoon period! Which brings me to the point of this letter. Thank you for helping to bring to completion what was started on New Year's Day.

Regards,

Nigel.

3

The Structure of Alpha

A is for anyone

That is, anyone interested in finding out more about the Christian faith. This includes at least five categories of people.

1. Those who are not Christians. Alpha is an evangelistic course, designed primarily for people who would not call themselves Christians. In the UK, this constitutes about 50 per cent of the population.

2. Those who are not churchgoers. In the UK, for example, 92.5 per cent of the population are not regular churchgoers. These are the people we aim to attract. There is a very big pool in which to fish.

The excitement of Alpha is seeing people outside of the church coming to faith in Christ, being filled with the Holy Spirit, getting excited about Jesus and going out and telling their friends. The buzz and excitement come from seeing people's lives being changed by the power of God.

Alpha has a totally different feel when we get people from

categories one and two on the course. I have never experienced this myself, but I am told that if it is only Christians on the course, it can all become a bit negative. Sometimes the course ends up as a theological nit-picking discussion. It can all go slightly downhill, in a rather unhelpful way. All you need is one unchurched person, for example Fred, who is not a Christian, and then all the Christians behave themselves! Instead of wondering what is wrong with the talk theologically, they are all praying, 'Lord, I do hope that Fred understands that.' When Fred comes to faith in Christ, and as a result goes back to his wife and his family is reunited, there is such joy and excitement that Fred brings his friends on the next course, and so on.

3. Those who are new Christians. Alpha also works well with people who are new Christians. It ties in very well with other types of evangelism such as mass evangelism or personal evangelism. If someone has just come to faith in Christ through some other means, Alpha is a great place for them to put down the foundations of their Christian faith.

4. Those who want to brush up on the basics. There may be some people who have been going to church all their lives but feel they have never really grasped the basics of the Christian faith, or never really experienced the love of God for themselves. I heard Bob Buford, an American businessman who now runs *Leadership Network*, make an interesting point. He said, 'For many people, going to church is like going to a movie that is halfway through. Nobody ever tells them what happened in the first half of the movie.' Alpha is like the bridge which tells people what happened in the first half of the movie so that they can understand the rest of it.

5. *Those new to the church.* Many people are daunted by going to a new church. If it is a large church, they feel intimidated by the numbers and wonder how they can ever get to know anyone. If it is a small church, they might feel very visible and awkward, like a stranger walking into a family party. If they come on an Alpha course, by definition the vast majority of the people on the course are new to the church because they are new Christians, not Christians or not churchgoers. They get to know a group of people who, like them, are new to the church; they make friends and that makes it much easier when they start coming to church. It also introduces them to the values of the church.

L is for learning and laughter

We believe it is possible to learn about the Christian faith and have a great deal of fun at the same time. There is always a lot of laughter over the meals and in discussion groups. During the talks we try to introduce as much humour as we can. As we are English, it is mainly self-deprecating humour! At the beginning of every evening, during the notices, we always stand up and tell a joke.

Alpha has been running for over thirty years. Over those thirty years we have been collecting jokes. We now have a grand total of six jokes! We tell those six jokes over and over again. We are always very grateful to the hosts and helpers (who have heard those six jokes many times) and indeed the guests who laugh out of all proportion to the joke's merits or the joke-teller's ability.

Humour breaks down barriers and makes people feel relaxed. We are trying to avoid intensity, because intensity is very off-putting to people outside of the church. G. K. Chesterton wrote, in his book *Orthodoxy*:

> One settles down into a sort of selfish seriousness. One has to rise to a gay self-forgetfulness (to use an old fashioned sense of the word). Seriousness is not a virtue. It is really a natural trend or lapse into taking oneself gravely because it is the easiest thing to do. It is much easier to write a good *Times* leading article than a good joke in *Punch*. Solemnity flows out of people naturally but laughter is a leap. It is easy to be heavy, hard to be light.

P is for pasta or potatoes or paella or pizza

Pasta is not a theological term, although in a sense it is. Someone said to me, 'There is something almost sacramental about the meal on Alpha.' As Robert Jenson wrote, 'All meals are intrinsically religious occasions, indeed sacrifices, and were so understood especially in Israel. . .sharing a meal is therefore always a communal act of worship and establishes fellowship precisely before the Lord.'[21] The meal on Alpha has a profound significance because it is over the meal that friendships are formed.

H is for helping one another

It is amazing to watch a group of people from outside the church changing over the course of ten weeks. There are many factors involved. We would like to think that the key factors are our talks or the gifts of the hosts and helpers, but very often it is the guests themselves who are helping one another.

I think of a group I had – a typical Alpha group, none of whom were churchgoers. They were all negative for the first few weeks. There was a guy called Matthew. Matthew had been dragged along by his wife, who was not a Christian – in fact she was Jewish. But she was very interested in going on the Alpha course, and he had been to chapel at school but had not been to church since. So she dragged him along. And he was the most negative person. He was negative really until about Week 5.

Everybody else was being negative that night, and Matthew hadn't said anything. So I turned to Matthew and I said, 'Matthew, what do you think?' He said, 'Well, it happened to me.' So I said, 'What happened to you?' He said, 'I shook on my bed in the middle of the night for three hours.' The other people in the group thought this was the funniest thing they had ever heard – Matthew shaking on his bed for three hours in the middle of the night – they fell off their chairs they were laughing so hard.

When they had picked themselves up from the floor, they said, 'What do you mean, you shook for three hours on your bed in the middle of the night?' He said, 'Well, it's like this: the other night, I couldn't sleep. So I thought I'd try that prayer that you pray. I repented of my sins, I thanked Jesus for dying for me and I asked him to come and fill me with the Holy Spirit, and then I shook for three hours!'

The other people were on the edge of their seats! Within ten days every single person in that group had come to faith in Christ. I remember them on the Alpha weekend, arms around each other, praying for each other. Matthew had helped the others.

A is for ask anything

Alpha starts with an A and ends with an A that stands for Ask Anything. No question is regarded as too simple. We find that older people are sometimes embarrassed by how simple their questions are. No question is too hostile. Some of the people who come on the course are very angry. That is fine. We want people who are angry, confused or antagonistic to come – that is who the course is designed for.

A TYPICAL EVENING

Most courses run in the evening, but there are highly effective courses running in the morning or at lunchtime (see Appendix C). These run in different venues: churches, homes, schools, offices, prisons, night clubs and restaurants. The guests range from mothers with young children to university students, from city high-flyers to gangs on estates, from prisoners to police officers.

Alpha can run at different times of day, but the most typical is the evening course.

6.30 pm	Hosts and helpers meet to pray
7.00 pm	Supper
7.40 pm	Welcome
7.50 pm	Songs of worship

8.00 pm	Talk (see Appendix A for list of talks and suggested order)
8.50 pm	Coffee
9.00 pm	Small groups
9.30 pm	Finish

At 6.30 pm we meet to pray and prepare. The meeting of the hosts and helpers at the beginning of the evening for prayer and organisation is of great importance. We have found that prayer is the key to everything that happens on Alpha. We encourage people to pray on their own; we also have a prayer meeting early on a Tuesday morning and, critically, we get together to pray just before the guests arrive on the evening itself. We have been particularly helped by Jeremy Jennings, who has put together a resource in a book called *The Church on its Knees*, which suggests new models of praying together that have inspired young people in particular to come together and pray.

At this meeting it is helpful to run through the evening, focusing on the subject matter and considering helpful questions for the small groups. It is also a time to deal with administration, particularly for the Holy Spirit weekend and celebration supper.

At 7.00 pm supper is served. When Alpha was small (around twelve) each person on the course took it in turns to cook supper (starting with the hosts and helpers). As it grew we reached a point where we had over ten small groups. Each small group then took it in turns to cook supper. This system was totally restructured when we reached over 200 and had to employ a caterer and ask the guests for a small contribution to cover the costs. If they cannot afford to contribute, they are still welcome to have the meal.

Eating together is an essential part of the course, as it gives people the chance to get to know others in a relaxed way. Friendships grow over the course, especially within the small group, in an extraordinary way. We have found that it is better to use the meal time to talk to the guests about the things they are interested in: their work, their leisure, their hobbies and sporting interests – anything, in fact, apart from religion!

At 7.40 pm we welcome everyone and give out notices, as well as advertising books from the recommended reading list and the CD of the previous week's talk. Towards the end of the course, we also use this time to talk about the weekend and the supper party. Then we tell the all-important joke.

At 7.50 pm we have a short period of singing. We explain carefully what we are going to do. I often quote what the apostle Paul says in his letter to the Ephesians: 'Speak to one another with psalms, hymns and spiritual songs. Sing and make music in your heart to the Lord' (Ephesians 5:19). I explain that we are going to sing a mixture of psalms (usually set to modern tunes), hymns and spiritual songs. We have a mixture of old and new. We always start the first night with a well-known hymn for the benefit of those who might find that more familiar. As the course goes on we tend towards more modern songs, changing gradually from singing about God to singing directly to him, and we increase the length of time we spend in worship from about five minutes on the first night to about fifteen to twenty minutes towards the end of the course. We try not to move too quickly at the beginning and I explain that what matters is that we 'sing and make music in our hearts'. Some may not be ready to participate, and it is fine for them simply to listen until they are ready to join in.

The worship leader must sound confident, even if he or she is not. We have found that it is better that the worship leader gives no introduction to the songs. He or she is there to lead worship rather than to give what can easily become another talk. Unless worship can be led and music played competently it is probably better not done at all. Some Alpha courses run without any singing. It is not an essential part of the course. The very small courses where guests listen to CDs or watch DVDs would not normally have any singing. However, people running a small- or medium-sized course have found that it is enriching to play a worship CD as backing if they do not have a worship leader, and this approach also works well (see Appendix H).

I have found that although many find the singing the most difficult part of the course to begin with, and some are even hostile towards it, by the end they often find it is the part they value most. For many, such singing is their first experience of communicating with God. It also helps people to make the step from Alpha to the church, where the worship of God is central.

After the singing we have the talk. This may be given by a host or helper who has the appropriate gifts and the time to prepare the material. We have produced the whole course on DVD, which some people prefer to use. Some course leaders find it distances them from the material, and enables the guests to be more open and honest in their response to the talk! Others find that there is simply too much else to think about, and that time saved preparing talks enables them to organise the administration and pastoral care more effectively. They may go on to do the talks themselves at a later date.

In the long term, we would recommend a live speaker doing the talks, but the DVD provides an effective second best. It is useful if the guests follow the talks by using an *Alpha Course Manual*, although they should not be charged for these. It is very important that people should hear the gospel free of charge. On a large course it is necessary to have someone who is used to and gifted at speaking to more sizeable gatherings. This inevitably limits the number of speakers available.

(In the next few paragraphs, when referring to a chapter in the book *Alpha – Questions of Life*, [22] which is based on the Alpha talks, I will use the abbreviation QL followed by the chapter number.)

The first week the talk is on 'Who Is Jesus?' (QL 2). In weeks two to six we cover the material in chapters 3–7. At this point we often have a weekend away. If we do, then the talk on week seven is, 'How Can I Resist Evil?' (QL 11). If the weekend away is at any other time, 'How Can I Resist Evil?' would follow it. This is because I have found that the talk about spiritual warfare only becomes really relevant after people have experienced the power of the Holy Spirit.

On week eight we look at 'Why and How Should I Tell Others?' (QL 12). At this stage, I start to talk about the supper party at the end of the course. The following week we look at the subject of healing (QL 13). There are no small groups that night as we stay together for ministry (see Chapter 13 in this book).

On the final night we look at the subject of the church (QL 14). The main aim of this talk is to start integrating those who have been on Alpha into the life of the church. We explain how the home group system in the church works and encourage them to join such a group. Often the whole small group on Alpha will join the same home group.

At the end of the talk we go into small groups (see Chapter 9 in this book) and aim to finish at 9.45 pm. It is tempting to run over time if the discussion is going well, but it is generally a bad idea. If the evening ends in the middle of a lively debate, the group tends to feel motivated to return next week. Conversely, if the group ends late, it becomes a reason to drop out after a long day at work.

The Alpha weekend

The weekend away is a crucial part of the course. This is the time that we devote to teaching on the work of the Holy Spirit in the individual lives of those on the course. The material covered is in chapters 8, 9, 10 and 15 of *Alpha – Questions of Life*. It is possible to cover this material in a single day. Sometimes we have a Saturday locally for those who cannot make one of the weekends. However, there are enormous advantages to the weekend away.

We have found that friendships are formed on a weekend much more easily than on a single day. As people travel together, have meals together, go for walks, enjoy the evening entertainments and receive Holy Communion together on Sunday morning, there is a cementing of the friendships which have begun to form in the early weeks. In this relaxed environment people start to unwind and some of the barriers begin to come down. I have found many make as much progress spiritually during the weekend away as in the rest of the course put together.

I know that it is hard to find a venue, but it is usually possible if plans are made far enough ahead. It may be worth combining with other churches in the area. If members of the congregation cannot afford to go away, then the weekend could take place in a local venue. However, in most congregations it is possible for those who can afford to pay to help those who cannot afford to pay anything at all or only a part. We always encourage people to attend the weekend whether they can afford to pay or not, as it is such a crucial element in the course, and we have always found that the financial arrangements resolve themselves. On the Sunday morning of the weekend, we have a collection, and assure people they are free to put in nothing, or as much or little as they would like. We then pray that God would be faithful to his promise to 'supply all your needs according to his riches in Christ Jesus' (Philippians 4:19). We are amazed by God's faithfulness.

The timetable for our weekend is as follows:

Friday

6.30 pm onwards	Arrive
8.00–10.00 pm	Supper
9.45 pm	Worship and a short introduction to the weekend – this can include a brief talk based on John 15 or perhaps a testimony.

Saturday

8.30 am	Breakfast
9.00 am	Hosts' and helpers' meeting
9.30 am	Worship
	Talk 1 – 'Who Is the Holy Spirit?'
10.45 am	Coffee
11.15 am	Talk 2 – 'What Does the Holy Spirit Do?'
12.00 noon	Small group discussion. Often we look at 1 Corinthians 12:7–11 and the subject of spiritual gifts. It is vital to make time to talk about

the gift of tongues during this small group discussion. People may be prompted by the passage to discuss their confusion and fears on the subject. Sometimes, one member of the group is able to share a positive experience, for example how the gift helped them to pray, or even just a real desire to experience the gift. Whatever people say, it is a good opportunity to get the subject in the open, and helps people feel much more comfortable when the gift of tongues is discussed on Saturday evening.

1.00 pm	Lunch
Free afternoon	Activities can be organised, eg, sports, walks etc.
4.00 pm	Optional tea
5.00 pm	Worship
	Talk 3 – 'How Can I be Filled with the Holy Spirit?'
7.00 pm	Supper
8.30 pm	Entertainment. A variety of sketches and songs without anything distasteful, religious or nasty. We have found that the entertainment contributes to people's enjoyment of the weekend, but only if they realise participation is entirely voluntary! It is extraordinary to uncover hidden gifts, and many who contribute suddenly become more confident and more 'part of things', and the course gains unity and momentum.

Sunday

9.00 am	Breakfast
9.20 am	Hosts' and helpers' meeting

9.45 am	Small group discussion. An opportunity for each guest to talk about what they have seen and heard so far. The feel of the group will probably have changed: objective questions often give way to subjective experiences as people share their responses, and may start to open up at a new level.
10.30 am	Worship Talk 4 – 'How Can I Make the Most of the Rest of My Life?' Holy Communion
1.00 pm	Lunch
Free afternoon	Hopefully everybody meets again at the evening service at church

Sometimes people say, 'We love Alpha! We think Alpha is fantastic! We love the idea of the meal, the discussion groups, the series of talks and so on. We love everything about Alpha – except the bit about the Holy Spirit. Could we run Alpha without the Holy Spirit?' Now, I know what they mean – they don't quite mean that. They mean without the weekend and the part about the person and the work of the Holy Spirit.

The answer is that it would not be Alpha. I often think it would be like a car that looks the same but is without an engine. One denomination did a survey of all the churches that were running Alpha, and they found there were a handful of churches where Alpha was not working. There were also a handful of churches that had cut out the weekend or the day on the Holy Spirit. They were the same churches.

Some people say, 'Well, we wouldn't do that, but what we would like to do is take out the bit about speaking in tongues. Could we leave that out?'

When we first went to the United States to do a conference there, a church growth expert came to see me and said, 'Look, if you cut out the bit about speaking in tongues, I could get Alpha running in all these denominations and streams . . . but you do need to cut that bit out.' I wondered whether he was right. Perhaps that shouldn't be part of the course. We thought about it carefully. All the way through we had seen the providence of God and also we had seen the effect on our course of this subject's inclusion. We did not feel it was right to omit it.

About a year later we were doing a conference in Nashville, Tennessee. Right at the start of the conference a Pentecostal pastor from Columbus, Ohio, came up to talk to me. He was so excited. He said, 'We have just run our first Alpha course. We didn't allow anyone to come unless they brought a friend from outside the church, and we had seventy-five people on the course.' He told us amazing stories about what had happened.

I said, 'Tell me: what did you find difficult as a Pentecostal running Alpha?' He replied, 'Well, we found the ministry difficult.' He was talking about the prayer ministry. I said, 'Don't you have prayer ministry in the Pentecostal church?' He said, 'Oh yes, we have prayer ministry in our church. But the style is very different. In our particular church when we have ministry we like lots of noise! We have a band, we have loud noise and we have lots of shouting!' He went on, 'When you ask the Holy Spirit to come, you only ask him quietly. We didn't think the Holy Spirit would come if we only asked him quietly! But we decided to try it, and he came!'

I said, 'Well, was there anything else you found difficult as a Pentecostal running Alpha?' He said, 'Yes, tongues.' I replied, 'I am so sorry, I thought you said that you were a Pentecostal!' He said, 'You don't have *enough* about the gift of tongues. It is only one third of one talk – one forty-fifth of the Alpha course. If you see Alpha as we do, as a two-year programme of adult Christian education, it is only one two-hundred-and-forty-fifth of the two-year programme! This is the only time that it is mentioned.'

On Alpha we say that you can be a Christian and filled with the Spirit and not speak in tongues. We don't believe there is such a thing as 'first-class Christians who speak in tongues and second-class Christians who don't'. We say that it is not the most important gift – in fact Paul often put it at the bottom of the list of gifts. Sometimes, people ask why we mention it at all in that case. Our answer is because we believe that both in the New Testament and also in experience it is often the first of the more obviously supernatural gifts of the Spirit that people begin to experience. The gift of tongues is a beginners' gift. Alpha is a course for beginners.

This Pentecostal pastor then said, 'You don't insist on the gift and you don't have enough material on it,' but he added, 'We were willing to "bend in love" and run it the way you do.' I remember thinking, 'Isn't that amazing?'

There may be other parts of the worldwide church at the opposite end of the spectrum who say, 'Well, we wouldn't have anything at all about it, but maybe we can just "bend a little bit in love" and do it the way that you do.' As a result all over the world there are Catholics, Protestants and Pentecostals all running the same course. We believe that could only be the providence of God.

The story of
Martin Bennett

4

Martin Bennett

*From the age of twelve, Martin Bennett was the victim of a
man who gave him drink, abused him and forced him to keep
everything secret. It went on for almost a decade. Here Martin
tells the effect that had on his life and how God lifted the 'terrible burden of guilt' and one afternoon changed his life.*

I was brought up a Catholic, but thought that God was something that you may come across when you're dead. I wasn't too
sure. As time went on, my attitude changed and I became very
anti-God, anti-Jesus and anti-religion.

When I was around twelve years old, I was abused by a teacher
in my school. He was a Catholic teacher, a single man and a high-
profile member of the local church. It all went on for a number of
years.

He used to get me very drunk. The first time I remember drinking Scotch was when I was at his place and he used to do things to
me when I was drunk, a lot of which I can't remember. I think
that's partly me blocking it out. He was an alcoholic. I can't
remember many times when I'd be with him when I wasn't

81

drinking or drunk. He put me in a position where I couldn't get out, and made me imagine that everything I did was wrong but that it was supposed to be kept secret. If I told other people about it then that would be very bad indeed. He would tell me secrets, confiding in me about other teachers, about other people in the community. I was therefore forced into a situation where I was emotionally attached to him when I didn't want to be. My way around it was to switch off my emotions completely.

I left that school when I was thirteen and went to secondary school so I got away from him in the school environment but in fact it got worse. As I got older, he'd take things away from me that I would need. It would start with things like my train pass. It might be money, my passport or anything like that. He'd take them away if I didn't contact him. So I would have to contact him and then the whole cycle would start up again. I was always covering my tracks – leading a double life in fact – from very early on. He was perceived to be a fine, upstanding member of the community. My parents did not know what was going on. Half the time they knew I was with him and that was acceptable to them because they still thought we had an OK relationship. No one knew what was going on, although I suspect my brothers had an inkling but were scared to come near it. I think they were frightened to think this could be happening. And I would have denied it to the ends of the earth.

I got to the stage in my early twenties when I still hadn't completely broken free from it. I was still seeing him off and on, but it wasn't with the same intensity. I knew I had to try and get away. I travelled around the world for two years or so, and he used to track me down in Australia and things like that. As a result of all this –

and I do connect the two very strongly – I grew very dependent on alcohol at an early age. I was drinking to make life easier and to try and forget things because I realised that if I drank enough, everything became a bit of a blur. It blocked things out of my mind. This continued for many years. I was drinking heavily from about sixteen or seventeen. The whole business was a huge great lead weight and I assumed that I'd carry that around with me always.

After I came back from travelling, I got involved with drugs. When I was twenty I was hospitalised for quite long periods of time with attacks of acute pancreatitis, which can be an alcohol-related disease. When I had these attacks I was given high levels of pethidine, which is a very strong painkiller to which I became addicted. I was told not to drink but this also became part of my double life as everyone assumed I wasn't drinking and all the time I was. It was part of my life that went into the 'secret file'. Most of the time I would go to sleep quite drunk.

I started off drinking a small amount of Scotch or vodka every day, but ended up drinking an awful lot by the end. It was usually vodka because I had heard people say you can't smell vodka. But if you wake up the next morning still drunk it doesn't matter what you've been drinking. During my longest stay in hospital, at the Middlesex, they were giving me Heminevrin to help with the alcohol withdrawal, pethidine to help with the pain . . . and I was drinking at the same time.

I had been going out with a girl called Catherine for a while and she realised something serious was going on. Eventually, it all came to a head, and thank God it did. I was twenty-six years old. I went to see various psychiatrists, psychologists, psychoanalysts, psychotherapists. Some were OK; some were awful; some were useless. I was still very reluctant to let everything out, but it was obvious to everyone that I was an alcoholic, so I went to a detoxification centre for about three months down in Epsom.

When I was at the detox centre, the story of the schoolteacher and what he had done began to come out. I never wanted anyone to know about it. I didn't want to tell the police and I didn't want a big thing made of it. But when people said, 'What if he's doing it to someone else?', then I felt morally obliged to talk to the authorities. As far as I know he was never prosecuted. But he's not teaching any more and he can never teach again.

Then I went to a halfway house in Queenstown Road, Battersea, and that was good. I had stopped drinking and that was great. I was really making progress. Catherine stood by me throughout this time. She was my constant source of strength and support. Without her I don't know what would have happened. Our relationship was obviously an awful lot better because I had stopped drinking. But there were still a lot of things that weren't right. I had the odd relapse with alcohol and these were very difficult times for Catherine. We got married in July 1992 and at that stage I hadn't been in hospital for a few years. We were married in a church, as both our parents were Catholic and it just seemed the right thing to do. (I didn't really get married in church for any other reason.) At the time, I was working for a film company as a camera technician.

Then in November Catherine heard from her cousin about the Alpha course at Holy Trinity Brompton. She thought she'd go along and see what it was like and so tagged on to the last half of the current course and she thought it was really great. I thought she was getting involved in some sort of cult and was a little bit concerned. However, she's a very sensible girl and so I thought that it couldn't be anything particularly bad. None the less it was certainly nothing that *I* wanted to get involved in. I would argue with Catherine a lot. My inbred dislike for any religion came out and it got to the stage where she wouldn't mention it to me any more because she knew I would want to argue.

Then Catherine got her cousin Madeleine, with her husband Con, her brother Michael, her sister Clare, her sister Anna and Anna's boyfriend, Tim, all to do the next Alpha course which started in January 1993. So they'd troop off every Wednesday night, and then went off to the weekend away and came back on an incredible high. Of course it was just emotionalism to me. I was still very, very cynical about the whole thing. Catherine would go off to church on Sundays and for a time she would ask me if I would come to church. I always used to refuse, but then after a while I stopped to think about it. There was such a change in Catherine.

She seemed to have an inner peace. I thought, 'I'm married to her. I really ought to check this out because if I don't, I won't know if I've missed anything.' So I came along to Holy Trinity Brompton on a Sunday evening and the first time I came I thought, 'Gosh, what a bunch of wallies.' But the one thing that stuck in my mind was the worship. Ric Thorpe was the worship leader then and I saw in him someone very much like myself. He just seemed a normal person. Every time he got up on the stage he looked like he was still laughing from a joke that someone had told him before he got up. I thought, 'I want to know what that joke is all about. I want to know why he looks so happy. And why are all these people so happy?'

So I went along the next week on the strength of that, and Catherine prayed (I didn't know this until later on) that I'd be touched by the Holy Spirit during the service. And I was. I didn't realise what it was at the time but I just felt this incredible peace come over me. During the worship, I broke down in tears. I was sitting down and everyone else was standing up and I was crying, crying my eyes out and I couldn't work out what was going on. I was in floods of tears. I couldn't stop it. I put it down to emotionalism and getting a bit caught up in the event. I was still quite anti-Holy Trinity Brompton but I decided I would do the Alpha course to give it a chance.

I went along to the first Alpha evening and agreed with most of the things I heard about the historical evidence of the existence of Jesus and the Bible and I thought, 'Yes, that's pretty good. I don't believe it, but that's pretty good.' But, I thought, 'If I'm going to get any benefit from this, I ought to discuss it with someone and try to clear away some of the cobwebs.' So I decided to ring Nicky Gumbel the next day. I said to myself, 'I'm going to try ringing him twice and if I don't get to speak to him then that's it. I will have tried.' I rang the first time and he was out and I thought, 'This is looking good.' I rang the second time and he was there and said, 'Yes, come along and see me today at 5.30 pm.'

So it was that on a summer's evening, 6th May 1993, at 5.30, I went along to Nicky's place. We went into his back garden and he said to me, 'Tell me a bit about yourself.' And I told him my life story. What was strange was I told him everything in one go which I'd never really done before. I'd been to see psychiatrists and psychologists and bits and bobs had come out but I just sat there in that back garden in Clapham and it all came out. It all seemed to be coming out in surprisingly frank detail which had never really happened before, and after about half an hour, he said to me, 'Well, do you feel like praying?' And I said 'No, not really,' because I didn't. But he said, 'OK. You don't have to pray but I'm going to pray.' So I said, 'Fine. Carry on.' He prayed out loud for me and as he was praying I decided, 'OK. I'll close my eyes.'

And this incredible peace came down on me. It was an over-whelming presence of goodness. Everything seemed so safe. He just carried on praying and after a while he said, 'I feel a very strong presence of God. Do you feel it?' I said, 'Yes, I do as well.' I couldn't believe it! And he said, 'Well, look, I've got this prayer written down in *Why Jesus?* Do you think you're up to praying it now?' And I said, 'Yes, I think I am.' Everything was pointing in that direction for me. It was a prayer turning away from every-thing I knew that I'd done wrong and asking God to come into my life.

In it is the line that says, 'I forgive all those who have wronged me' – or words to that effect – and Nicky said to me that he wanted me to include the name of the guy who had abused me when I was younger and to say that I forgave him. This was quite a thing to me. The whole idea of forgiving him was totally beyond me, totally beyond my comprehension. But I said that I forgave this man. I said it three times, and each time my burden got lighter, so that by the third time I felt I was rising up into the trees. I felt an incredible release of this weight that had been dragging me down. It was lifted from me. I knew that I'd forgiven this per-son and that God had forgiven me. I had carried around all the guilt for a long, long time. It was quite incredible!

I opened my eyes again and there were tears pouring down my

face, and it was the same with Nicky. He said something to the effect that he never fails to be surprised and amazed by the power of God. And I said, 'Well, I agree!' What had happened to me was something that was amazing – so powerful, so relevant and so unique. There was nothing like that when I went to see any of the psychiatrists or whatever. There was no comparison. It was total cleansing. Total forgiveness is way, way beyond anything you'll ever find in a book; any sort of Jungianism or Freudianism or anything like that. They just pale into insignificance compared to forgiving, being forgiven and starting a relationship with Jesus.

We had a friend coming round for supper that evening and I wanted to tell Catherine what had happened. I saw our friend trying to park outside and so I ran out of the door shouting back to Catherine: 'I've just been round to see Nicky Gumbel and I've given my life to Christ.' And she thought, 'What!' But once she understood what I was saying she was delighted. It was lovely.

Incidentally, the fellow who came to dinner that night, who wasn't a churchgoer, has just done the Alpha course and is helping on the current Alpha course.

I went and told my mother the next day and I've never seen her happier. It was incredible. She had been praying for me for a long time. I drove down the A3 to my parents' house with tears streaming down my face listening to tapes of praise and worship music. I needed windscreen wipers on my eyes really. There were lots of tears of joy, happiness . . . Oh, unbelievable happiness. It was great!

My father, who is a more traditional Catholic, also recognised that something quite significant had happened to me. I wrote to my in-laws, who had also been praying, and they were very happy.

The following Sunday in church Sandy Millar invited anyone who wanted to receive the Holy Spirit up to the front. I went and, as I was prayed for, I felt the Holy Spirit rushing into me. He filled me up. I had been feeling a little bit vulnerable, but once I really felt I'd got the Holy Spirit on board I thought, 'I can cope with anything.' I had that power and that reassurance.

I carried on with the Alpha course and everything began making sense to me then. All my pseudo-intellectual arguments disappeared. All the cynicism went. It was incredible! I was happy! It has made such a difference to Catherine and our relationship. We have been to a few weddings since ours and the marriage vows spring out at me now. They mean so much more. We try to pray every day and have a prayer group with the people I met on my first Alpha course. I pray on occasions for the man who abused me. I've realised that he's obviously a very lonely, very mixed-up, very sad person. He's not a problem for me any more.

It has all been such an answer to prayer. Catherine was praying her head off during that time when she was going to Alpha without me. She had a prayer diary and we've been looking back at it. It's got things like 'Prayed that Martin does go to church.' That's got a tick by it. 'Prayed that Martin does the Alpha course.' That's got two ticks by it. 'Prayed that Martin becomes a Christian.' That's got a great huge tick by it, and lots of other ticks with a little smiley face!

5

The Alpha Recipe

In my last year at university, my wife Pippa (who was just a friend at that time) was working as a professional cook in Belgium. When we had friends around and needed to cook food I would often ask her for a recipe. We were students living on a fairly simple diet. We had cereal for breakfast and bread and cheese for lunch. We had a pint of milk delivered every day. We bought a loaf of bread and some cheese. When the bread reached a certain stage of staleness we would put it out on the window sill to dry out to become rusks. One time we had accumulated a lot of milk in our fridge and quite a lot of bread had been accumulated on our window sill. We also had one egg and a little cheese. So I rang Pippa and said, 'Is there a recipe that involves eggs, cheese, bread and milk?' She said, 'Yes, there is. Take twelve eggs, whisk them together, add a little bit of milk, then soak the bread in the mixture, put a little cheese on the top and place it in the oven and you will make a soufflé.' I thought, 'Great, sounds absolutely perfect! Well, it won't matter that our proportions are slightly different.' So I put in the one egg, the seven pints of milk, soaked the bread in

91

the milk, put a little cheese on top and stuck it in the oven. It was absolutely disgusting. It was inedible!

The problem was that I hadn't quite followed the recipe. I think sometimes people do the same with Alpha. They think, 'Oh, well, perhaps we will just change it around a bit and see what happens.' If people do that, the problem is that they will never know whether Alpha would have worked if they had run it according to the recipe. We recommend that churches follow the recipe, at least the first few times that they run it. It might just be that there is a reason why you need those twelve eggs and only a small amount of milk, rather than the other way round. But you will never discover unless you try it.

We have been running the Alpha course for over thirty years – and we have made so many mistakes. As a result of all those mistakes, we have come up with 'the Alpha recipe': the ingredients and methods which are most simple to use and have been tried and tested again and again. We would recommend following that recipe closely. So what is the recipe?

WHEN?

First, the dates need to be fixed. The course takes eleven weeks (including the party at the end). Alpha at Holy Trinity Brompton takes place on Wednesday evenings (although there is also a day-time Alpha course – see Appendix C). It is of utmost importance, in order to maintain the momentum, to run *at least* three courses a year. If this happens, then a guest can attend an Alpha course, come to faith in Christ, be filled with the Spirit, get excited about Jesus and ask their friends on the next course. Clearly there must be a next course to ask their friends to, so you do not want too big a gap between courses. We used to run four a year, but due to the size we have had to cut down to three. The best times are usually during the autumn term (October to December), spring term (January to April) and summer term (May to July).

Because Alpha is a rolling programme, and also because it takes a little bit of time to adjust to it, I really do not think we can know whether Alpha works for us until we have run it at least nine times! There are two reasons for this: when a church first starts Alpha, the guests tend to be church members and the courses are quite large. After a while, most of the church members have done the course and the size of the course falls correspondingly. It is only after three or four courses have been held that fringe members and non-churchgoers start filtering into the course and numbers start to rise again. This is when Alpha *actually* starts. One pastor from Kansas City came to an Alpha conference in an Anglican church in Toronto and went home saying, 'I am going to go back and run this course nine times, whether it works or whether it doesn't.' On his first course he had twenty people and they were all Christians – he found this part extremely boring! He had twelve people on the next course, but none of them were Christians. Within two years the course had grown to 125.

Alpha is not a quick-fix solution to church growth. However, if we want a long-term way to see people coming into the church, then I don't know of a more effective way than Alpha. The key is keeping going because it takes a number of times to de-bug it, to get used to it, to work out how it works for our situation. The vicar from one of our church plants told me recently that the break-through happened on their thirty-sixth Alpha course – so we need to persist!

WHERE?

A venue needs to be found. The ideal venue is a home. At Holy Trinity we had considerable hesitations about moving from a home after many years because such an environment is unthreatening for those who do not go to church. We only did so eventually because of the increasing size of the course. When the course outgrows the home, a venue with a welcoming atmosphere needs to be found.

HOW DO WE GET PEOPLE TO COME?

Fourteen ways to attract people to your Alpha course
Encouraging people to attend the Alpha course is a hurdle that many churches find difficult to cross. Most people attend the course because they have been invited personally by a friend or family member, yet there are many ways of reaching out into the wider community and encouraging people to attend.

1. Friends, family and work colleagues of those who did a previous course. The main way a course will grow is by people who have attended Alpha telling their friends, family and work colleagues about their experience and inviting them on a subsequent course. The more we run Alpha the more this builds. Some of those who have just completed a course may ask their friends on the next course, but equally they may ask them in a year's time or even in three years' time. This underlines the importance of running Alpha as a rolling programme.

One of the aims of the talk 'Why and How Should I Tell

Others?' (Week 8) is to motivate the guests from our current course to invite their friends to the Alpha celebration supper and the next Alpha course.

2. Alpha celebration suppers. The purpose of the Alpha celebration supper is both to celebrate the end of one Alpha course and to launch the next course. It provides an easy way for guests to invite friends, family and work colleagues to come and hear the talk 'Is There More to Life Than This?' in a friendly environment. As part of the Alpha Initiative, supper invitations have been produced. People can use these to invite their friends.

We aim to create an environment which is relaxed and non-threatening. It should have the feel of a celebration party. We put out tablecloths, flowers, candles, and have music (not worship songs) playing in the background.

A suggested timetable is as follows:

7.00 pm	Guests arrive
7.15 pm	Supper
8.30 pm	Interviews
8.50 pm	Talk – 'Is There More to Life than This?'
9.25 pm	Coffee
9.30 pm	People start to leave

The testimonies are a very important part of the evening (see the Appendices for suggestions on how to choose people and run the interview).

We suggest that copies of *Why Jesus?*[23] and invitations to the next course are available on the tables during coffee or dessert and/or as they leave at the end of the evening. We do not ask people to sign up for the course that evening as we find people prefer to remain anonymous. I suggest that they come along to the first night of Alpha, and assure them that if they don't want to come back, no one will ring them up or send them junk mail. This takes the pressure off them. Most who come to the first night continue to come of their own accord.

3. Congregation contacts. On average, a church of 100 people will have 300 family contacts and any number of friends, colleagues and acquaintances. Research shows that the church door is a big barrier for many people. However, a personal invitation to an Alpha course by someone they know can be very attractive. This is one of the reasons why it is so important for the parish priest, minister, pastor, elder (ie the person who is leading the church) to be pro-actively encouraging the congregation to bring their friends.

I have a friend called Wes Richards, who is the pastor of an independent church in Slough. They have been running Alpha for a number of years, very successfully. They have had about seventy people coming to their celebration suppers. The course has run very well. Eighteen months ago he decided that they were going to change tack in this sense. Alpha is now part of their DNA. They were going to make it a central plank in their evangelistic strategy and he was really going to push it. He encouraged the congregation to bring their friends. He preached about it. That September the numbers went up from seventy at the celebration suppers to 700.

4. Baptism candidates. Most churches have a personal fringe, but they also have an institutional fringe – that is to say, people who relate to the church as an institution. For example, in many parts of the church there are couples who bring their children for baptism. We have found that Alpha is an ideal course to offer as preparation for parents who wish to have their children baptised.

5. Engaged couples. Many people start coming to church services because they want to get married. Why not encourage those who are planning to marry in your church (or who are recently married) to attend the Alpha course?

One church leader attended an Alpha conference and returned home full of enthusiasm. He spoke about Alpha in the service the following Sunday and none of the congregation showed the slightest interest. He went home very discouraged. But he prayed. Then he thought, 'I have married five young couples this year, and none of them are Christians or come to church. I will invite them.' He did, and four out of the five said they would come. They had a great time. Several gave their lives to Christ, three are now PCC members and one is the church treasurer.

6. Occasional churchgoers. Many people go to church at Christmas, Easter, Harvest festival or for family services. These are ideal opportunities to reach out to those who may not normally come to church. An appropriate talk may refer to the Alpha course, or we might advertise via the notice boards or other forms of publicity. At Christmas, for example, we give away copies of *Why Christmas?* (with an invitation to the next Alpha course) at the end of the service.

7. The church magazine. If you have a church or community magazine, use it to publicise your course. Printing interviews with those who have come to Christ on the local Alpha course has proved a very effective method of encouraging others to come along. This method may reach those who only have contact with the church through the church magazine. If you have not already run an Alpha course, it might be useful to use testimonies from other churches or stories from *Alpha News* or the book *The God Who Changes Lives.* (Please contact the Communications Office at Holy Trinity Brompton to obtain permission.)

8. Community groups (scouts and guides, mother and toddler groups, marriage and parenting courses). A number of churches are now involved in community activities. Drop-ins for the homeless, coffee mornings for mothers and toddlers and marriage and parenting courses are increasingly popular with non-churchgoers. These provide the ideal setting to mention or even run the Alpha course.

9. Guest services. Guest services are aimed specifically at non-churchgoers and can be held on the Sunday before the Alpha course starts. We make sure that the date of the service is published in good time and encourage the regular members of our church to bring their friends. The service is broadly similar to a normal Sunday service and the key is to make it as non-threatening and welcoming as possible. Many people come on Alpha as a result of attending a service like this.

Personal stories of changed lives are a key element of guest services. They are a powerful way of encouraging people to come on Alpha and are very easy to arrange. We try to find people who would be attractive to our guests – people with 'street cred'. If you haven't run Alpha before, perhaps ask someone from another church to come and give their testimony. We don't give them too much notice – testimonies are often most effective when they are spontaneous. We use an interview style, and keep the interview questions simple.

We use three very basic questions along these lines:

- Were you a Christian/churchgoer six months ago?
- What happened?
- And what difference has Jesus made in your life?

It is a good idea to promote the service with printed invitations or even an advertisement in the church magazine or local newspaper. We would also recommend having an 'Alpha team' present at the end of the service to answer questions and hand out invitations to the next Alpha course with copies of *Why Jesus?*

10. Alpha Sundays. An Alpha Sunday is usually held the week before the guest service, and is a normal Sunday service with a ten-minute slot about Alpha. It aims to encourage members of your congregation to invite their friends to the guest service the following week and to your next Alpha course. This usually takes the form of a brief explanation of what the course entails and a couple of testimonies from the last course. We hand out an invitation to the forthcoming Alpha course with the service sheets and publicise the guest service, which will take place the following week, to remind the congregation to bring their friends.

11. Missions and evangelistic events. Alpha is an ideal follow-up course for a mission and has been used in this way by Luis Palau,

J. John and other evangelists. If you have a local mission event, church fête or other community activity in your area, you could use the Alpha course as a follow-up to the event, encouraging all those at the event to explore the Christian faith further at an Alpha course in their local church. It is good to ensure that details of local Alpha courses are available at the event.

12. Family life courses. Increasingly, we are finding that these courses are providing a source of new people. Some people would not come on an Alpha course but they know they need help with their marriage or with parenting, for example. Nicky and Sila Lee run a marriage course at Holy Trinity Brompton in a similar way to the Alpha course in the sense that people come and have a meal, hear a talk, have coffee and go into small groups. The only difference is that the small group has two members: a husband and a wife. They have various exercises that they work through together. It has proved very successful with people outside the church. Increasingly, I think, people are recognising that marriage is one of the really important things that we do that we get no training for in our society and we need help. It is not an admission of failure to go on a marriage course. Actually, it is a sensible thing to do – even if a marriage is very successful, it could be more successful, it could always be better.

We get people at all stages – people whose marriages are very good right through to people who are on the brink of divorce – coming on the course. Often at the end, they say, 'We love this. We really enjoyed it.' Maybe, during the course they heard a little bit about Alpha and they say, 'Now we would like to do an Alpha course.' We always have a number of people on Alpha who have come from the marriage course. Now it is also two-way traffic: there are people who come on Alpha who say, 'We need help with our marriage.' So they are going from the marriage course to Alpha and from Alpha to the marriage course.

13. The Alpha Directory. This is a list of churches that are running Alpha. There is no charge for going into the directory. We have found that it is an enormous help for people who want to recommend Alpha to their friends, family and work colleagues who may live in a different part of the country.

We would highly recommend registering your Alpha course if you have not yet done so. This means that your details automatically go on the Alpha website. An increasing number of people are attending Alpha courses on the recommendation of relatives or friends in another part of the country or the world, who have referred to the directory in *Alpha News* or at the Alpha Office.

One young man wanted his father-in-law, a window cleaner in Weston-super-Mare, to go on Alpha. So he looked in the Alpha Directory to see where the nearest church running a course was, and took his father-in-law along to the first evening. He loved it and completed the rest of the course. He became a Christian, and as a window cleaner is a very effective evangelist!

14. Caring for Ex-Offenders (CFEO). Twenty-two thousand people have done the Alpha course in prison. Large numbers of them are now coming out of prison and are being reintegrated into the local Christian community through the CFEO ministry. We have found that CFEO is a very effective way of inviting people, especially aged eighteen to thirty-five, on the Alpha course.

We have sixteen ex-offenders in our own congregation, and it has been such a blessing to witness the transformation in their lives. These sixteen have invited huge numbers of their friends onto the Alpha course and to our church. Several of them have helped on Alpha and a few have been regular members at our church for a long time

15. *Using promotional resources*

- Church notice boards – It is a widely held opinion in the advertising business that churches have the greatest under-used advertising resource: church notice boards on main roads up and down the country.
- Posters – Posters in the windows of church members' homes are a good source of free advertising and will let all the neighbours know about Alpha. If every person who had done Alpha in the UK (over 2 million people) were to put posters up in their windows, that in itself would have a major impact. Posters can also be placed in shop windows, libraries, pubs, coffee shops, offices and factories – with permission!
- Car stickers – This is a relatively inexpensive way of providing advertising.
- Leaflets to homes – Recently a church in Ealing wanted to reach as many people as possible so they paid for a leaflet drop to 10,000 houses in their community at a cost of £200. As a result sixty-five unchurched people came to their Alpha supper, fifty of whom went on to do the course itself. Most of them had no Christian background whatsoever.
- Participate in the Alpha Initiative – Since the launch of Alpha

Initiatives in 1998, we have witnessed a noticeable rise in the number of people attending Alpha in those countries where the Initiative is run. In the UK there has been a doubling of the number of non-churchgoers attending the course and it is estimated that over 9 million people worldwide have now attended the Alpha course.

Most people attend an Alpha course as a result of a personal invitation. The role of advertising is to make the personal invitation easier. There are five benefits of advertising:

- It confers a sense of legitimacy. The average person concludes that something significant must be happening when they see extensive coverage of the course.
- Those who have done Alpha are encouraged to invite others because of the reinforcement of the media.
- It provides a conversation starter. Billboards, church notices or posters in people's homes make it easier to say, 'Oh, have you seen that billboard or poster? That's what we're running in our home this week. Would you like to come along?'
- If someone has received a leaflet, seen the billboards or posters and read about Alpha in the newspaper, it may plant the idea that they would like to go along. This makes them more likely to respond to the personal invitation.
- Advertising raises spiritual issues in the media and is likely to get people talking and make them more open to an invitation.

However, advertising does not work alone. It must be complemented by Christians actually inviting friends, family and colleagues to Alpha.

SELECTING A TEAM

When starting an Alpha course, the first task is to choose a leadership team. If the course is going to be a large one (thirty plus) the team will need to include an administrator and possibly a worship leader.

Approximately one third of the course members should be hosts and helpers. Each small group is made up of around twelve people of whom three or four are hosts and helpers. We have found that these people need to be selected very carefully. The hosts must be those who appear to have the beginnings of a gift of evangelism. They do not necessarily need to be Christians of many years' standing, but one indication of this gift is that they are 'good with people'. This is the test I often use when someone suggests someone, say Jane, as a host: 'Suppose you had a non-churchgoing friend for whom you had been praying for several years; would you be totally confident about putting them in Jane's group?' If the answer is 'No' Jane is probably not suitable to be a small group host on Alpha. If the answer is 'Yes' then Jane is likely to be a good host.

In every group we also have one or two helpers, usually one man and one woman. They might be a couple or two single people. We do, however, try not to have a boyfriend and girlfriend hosting or helping with a group, as complications can arise if the relationship breaks up halfway through the course. The ideal is to have one couple and two single people on the leadership team of each group.

The helpers should pass the same test as the hosts, but they may be relatively new Christians. Indeed, occasionally they may not even be Christians at all. Many of our helpers are those who have just finished the previous course. Some ask to come back and do the course again. In many cases we would ask them to come back as helpers. We strongly discourage anyone from simply repeating the course. We do not want people to get stuck doing Alpha over and over again – they need to move on in their journey of faith, and one of the ways of moving on is to come back and help others. People who have recently done the course are often especially sensitive to the fears and doubts of members in their group. They can empathise with them, saying, 'I felt that,' or, 'I found that difficult.' This removes the 'us' and 'them' barrier.

As well as those who request to come back, we ask the hosts of the previous course to recommend those from their small group who they think would be good at helping. I myself look out for those I think would make good helpers and ask them to come back and help. Many of them are new Christians and many have lots of friends who are not Christians. A group of 'happening' people attracts other people. Quite a high percentage of the next course will be friends of those who are helping. This is one of the ways in which the course grows. I have observed that those in the 18–35 age group generally have the largest groups of friends, and that many of them are still 'open-minded' about their worldview. We have found that once people from this age group come to a course, numbers seem to rise more quickly. If we are to attract young people, we will need hosts and helpers in their age group.

I met someone called Nan Kirkland, who is eighty years of age. Nan has run Alpha nine times and has had over 250 people going through the courses. She showed me a picture of her course, and my eyes were out on stalks when I saw it, because in a group of thirty people, no one was over thirty apart from Nan. I didn't want to ask a rude question, but I said, 'How did you get all these young people on the course?' She replied, 'Well, I will not have any hosts or helpers over thirty on my course . . . most of my hosts are twenty or twenty-one and they attract the others.'

Now, this doesn't mean to say that if we are over thirty there is nothing for us to do! Nan has proved that – she has got herself a job! But she has seen that if we want to attract the young people outside the church, we need young hosts and young helpers.

Some people do not have the appropriate gifts or personality to be hosts and helpers. At times, we can make the mistake of thinking it would help them, even if they would not be the right person to help the guests. This is upside down thinking – our focus should be our guests on Alpha. If people would not be suitable hosts or helpers, we have found it much more positive to suggest that their gifts be used in other areas of the course, for example on the 'taskforce'.

The taskforce is made up of a group of people who perform practical tasks such as catering, washing up and moving chairs. They are vital to the smooth running of the course. They do not take part in the small groups, as they are fully occupied with the practical tasks. We have a dynamic group on the taskforce. They are people who either do not want to be in a small group or would not be suitable for a small group but have 'the gift of helps' (1 Corinthians 12:28). They are like the group chosen in Acts to 'wait on tables' (Acts 6:2). They are men and women who are full of the Spirit and willing to serve in any capacity. Their love and service are in themselves a powerful witness to the love of Christ to those who are on the course.

A Catholic priest from one of the first Catholic parishes to run Alpha came to an Alpha conference at Holy Trinity Brompton. He went back and ran Alpha in his parish and it was a great success. I asked him whether he was giving the talks on the Alpha course, and he replied, 'No, I do not give the talks. I do not feel that is particularly my gift.' I went on, 'Are you hosting a group on the course?' and he said, 'No, I do not feel that is particularly me.' So I said, 'Are you involved?' and he said, 'Oh yes, I am involved. I cook the food and I clear up afterwards. That is what I feel my gifts are. I love to be involved, I love everyone to know that I am supporting it, but that is my gift.'

It showed extraordinary humility to be willing to do that. And I am not surprised to hear how well his course is working and how many people are coming to Christ through it. He loves Alpha because he sees people's faith in Christ coming alive and he enjoys using one of his gifts – I am sure he has many, many other gifts – and he loves watching other people using their gifts.

TRAINING THE TEAM

Our latest research has shown that 26 per cent of churches that are running Alpha do not run any team training. It breaks my heart to hear that! If the team is not trained, the small groups are very unlikely to work well. It is so sad to have gone to so much trouble to get the people there and then not to give them the best possible experience.

It is vital that all the team (especially those who have been Christians for many years) are trained each time we run an Alpha course. Hosts and helpers are invited to the training sessions. We run three evenings of training. Two are usually held on the two Wednesdays before the course begins. The first talk is on pastoral care (see Chapter 7). The second is on hosting a small group (see Chapter 9). The third training session is usually held on a Monday evening, just before the first weekend away. This session is on the subject of ministry (see Chapter 13). These training evenings are opportunities for the teams to get to know one another before the Alpha course starts and for them to get together to pray for the course.

On the training evenings we meet at 7.00 pm for supper. It is important that the team should spend time together and get to know each other before the course begins. We don't assume that they already know each other very well. At 7.45 pm we begin with worship and prayer. All the way through we stress the importance of praying for the course. We then have a talk and an opportunity to ask questions either relating to the talk or about any other aspect of the course. At this point we cover some of the administrative details and prepare people for the jobs they will be asked to do on the first evening and thereafter. We aim to finish each training session at 9.45 pm.

After Alpha

In practice, the strong friendships often formed on Alpha mean that the small groups want to stay together afterwards. However, new Christians need to be integrated into the life of the Christian community, and the appropriate ways of doing this will vary. With thousands of Alpha courses now running, there have been many requests for more follow-up material suitable for use in a pastorate or home group setting. In response to this, we are compiling a programme of adult Christian education which now includes the following: *Alpha – Questions of Life*, Term 2 *A Life Worth Living*, Terms 3–4 *Challenging Lifestyle*, Term 5 *Searching Issues*, and Term 6 *The Heart of Revival*.

These resources aim to give people solid biblical roots for their new faith and lifestyle, and to address problems and difficult issues in a clear and simple way.

CONCLUSION

Sometimes people ask me whether Alpha is always a success story. They want to know if every person who comes on the course becomes a Christian, is filled with the Spirit, gets excited about Jesus and brings hundreds of friends to the next course. Unfortunately the answer is, 'No, it's not always like that!' Surveys from recent courses have shown that approximately 25 per cent of the guests had dropped out. When we analysed why, we found the following reasons.

First they stopped coming because of us. We did not run the course as well as we might have done. For this reason we have questionnaires at the end of the course so that we can constantly improve it and make it more user-friendly. (See Appendix E.)

Second, people drop out for legitimate reasons. For example, some move to another part of the country. Increasingly, however, people are able to carry on the course where they move to. I know of one couple who started the course in London and finished it in Hong Kong! Another man did Weeks 1–7 at HTB, Week 8 in Boston, where he was on business, and then finished the course with us in London. This shows the advantage of the Alpha Directory.

Third, people drop out for reasons connected with the parable of the sower (Matthew 13:3–8, 18–23). Jesus said that some people's hearts are hard: they are simply not ready to hear and they may leave after the first evening. Sometimes they come back on the next course, or a year later. One person came back after four years and said to me, 'I have never forgotten what I heard the first night.'

Some drop out because of personal troubles in their lives, or through persecution or ridicule. Somebody may laugh at them and say, 'What are you doing going to church on a Wednesday?' Many of the people who come on the course lie about what they're doing on Wednesday nights. One man told me that a friend of his had come over from New Zealand and asked him out for a drink on a Wednesday night. As he was going to Alpha he gave a vague excuse: he was not prepared to admit what he was doing. So his friend said, 'Oh that's a pity,' and he looked through his diary, and asked, 'How about next Wednesday?' He explained that he was busy, but had difficulty justifying why he was busy the next Wednesday and the next. Finally he admitted to being on a course. 'What course is that?' the friend asked. 'Oh,' he replied, 'I am learning French.'

Jesus also outlines another category of people for whom the cares of this world, the delight in riches and the desire for other things come in and choke the word. We have found that a new relationship or success at work or some other distraction may take people away either during or even after the end of the course.

And that leaves the last category, which Jesus called the good soil. A recent Alpha group that I was involved in was, in some ways, extremely discouraging! By the end of the course, only one person remained, apart from the hosts and helpers. His name was David. He was a futures broker and a commuter, and had sat opposite the same man on the train for many years. Being English, they had never spoken to each other, as they had not been introduced! However, they met at a party, they were introduced, and ultimately David went to work for Nick. They were having lunch together one day, and David asked Nick how he coped in such a highly pressurised job. Nick replied, 'Actually, it's God.' The consequence of this conversation was that David came on the Alpha course.

One evening, about three or four weeks into the course, David had not said much. When someone asked him how he was, he explained that he had been for a medical in order to start his new job. The doctor had subsequently rung him to say that one of his liver counts was over ten times too high: he would die in six months if he didn't stop drinking. Only David's close family knew that he was an alcoholic, and his marriage was under a lot of strain. The group hosts offered to pray for David, for him to receive Christ and for his addiction to be broken. David was, in his own words, 'somewhat sceptical', but thought that anything was worth a try. The next day at work he was amazed to look at his watch and see that it was 2.00 pm. Previously, he would have felt an overwhelming desire for a drink by then, but this day there was nothing. The following week David explained what had happened. He said that each time he felt the emptiness that usually caused him to reach for a drink, he read his Bible. His wife was furious that he had done this for God when she had been asking him for twenty years! She did, however, come to the celebration supper, and brought their two children, aged twelve and fifteen. When I was chatting to her, she said that David was a different man: she now had a husband and the children had a father.

It was not difficult to persuade David's wife, Anne, to do the next course. The children got involved too, telling their schoolfriends what had happened to them. Next, David's sister did Alpha, having seen the change in her brother. Then a couple came on Alpha, simply because they had heard David's story. One helper brought her husband along, who was also an alcoholic, and he too was set free from alcoholism. Another couple, who had dropped out of the Alpha course, came back to see what had happened to David, and went on to complete another Alpha course. By now David and Anne's marriage had been totally transformed by the Holy Spirit. They then led an Alpha group together: not one person dropped out!

The seed that falls on good soil bears fruit thirty-fold, sixty-fold, or, in David's case, a hundred-fold.

The story of
Mary Stephenson

6

Mary Stephenson

Mary Stephenson's mother prayed all her life that her daughter might come to faith in Jesus Christ. She watched as Mary became a drug addict, a thief and eventually an inmate of Holloway Prison – but she never stopped praying. She died in 1987. Here Mary describes how her mother's prayers were finally answered.

When I was six weeks old, I was adopted from the Catholic Children's Adoption Society into a good home. My adoptive father was a diplomat and my mother was American. She was a devout Catholic and one of the things I truly believe is that it is through her prayers that I'm here today. I know that she prayed for me daily. I was raised in South America and when I was about ten I was sent to a convent boarding school in England. It was probably then that I started to get quite independent. It's not like being at day school where you can go home to Mum and tell her that you're upset about something. At boarding school I tended to sort out my problems myself. Sometimes I wouldn't see Mum and Dad for about four months.

I did my 'A' levels when I was seventeen. One of them was in theology, but I didn't read the New Testament, so I failed it. There seem to have been so many times when God has been in my life but I've ignored him completely because I had no understanding. Nobody explained God to me.

I was off like a shot when I finished school. I moved up to London straight away and got involved with what I thought was a great crowd. I went to all the parties and took something called 'smack' which somebody gave to me saying, 'Snort this. It's really fab.' So I snorted it up my nose and thought it was such a wonderful feeling. I remember telling a girlfriend of mine, 'You've got to try this. It's so good,' and she said, 'Mary! Smack is heroin.' I said, 'Don't be so daft.' Of course if somebody had handed me a syringe with a needle on the end and said, 'Try this,' I would have said, 'On your bike,' because I always thought that heroin, syringes, junkies and Piccadilly Circus went together. But I snorted this apparently quite harmless powder and it was such a nice feeling. I didn't understand what all the fuss was about.

However it all soon led to 'chasing the dragon' and then mainlining. I spent the next six or seven years leading a life of deceit, dishonesty, lying and whoring . . . complete abuse. My friends were doing it and I wanted to be involved. To start off with, I used to buy it from them, but as time went on I got to meet the dealers. I really did dive in, but I thought I was all right because I always had a job of some description. I was doing secretarial work at the time. I used to say: 'Well, all my other friends who are junkies are unemployed so I can't be that bad because I'm in work.' I still had to have a fix to get up in the morning and one at lunch time and one in the evenings. But I went to work and I didn't actually realise what sort of state I was in.

I think my brother, who was a medical student at the time, began to notice but I convinced myself that I was leading a normal life. Mum and Dad were abroad, so they didn't really know too much about it. I didn't go home because I never had any money. Occasionally they paid for me to come home and then I used to get quite sick because I was withdrawing. I remember my mother thinking I had rheumatic fever because I was aching and shivering all over. Every time that happened I used to tell myself that I was never going to touch the stuff again. Then, as soon as I got off the plane when I got back to London, I 'scored' straight away.

I became very dishonest and was stealing cheques and things. Inevitably I got caught and at my first court case my dad really put his career on the line because he stood up in court for me. Unfortunately, the press got hold of it because, although I was nobody, my father was an ambassador at the time. It really broke my parents' hearts and, although it wasn't their fault at all, they blamed themselves. I used to say, 'I'll be all right, Mum. I'll get my act together now.' Then as soon as they went off I'd go back to using.

I ended up in Holloway Prison because I got arrested for stealing. Dealers would acquire stolen cheque books and cheque cards and then they would say, 'You go out and buy this,' if it was a woman's cheque book and card. So I would pretend to be that person and buy whatever items the dealers wanted – or, more often than not, go into banks and cash the cheque, and get the cash for them – and they would give me drugs in exchange.

What goes on in prison is frightening. I have never been so terrified in my entire life. I couldn't believe what was happening. It's a very frightening and vicious circle and I am very glad that I was only in there for a short spell – about six to eight weeks.

I got out on the condition that I would go to a clinic for a year on probation. My parents took me up there and Mum said to the director, 'Where's the nearest Catholic priest or church because I want to contact them so that they know Mary's here?' The director said to Mum: 'Look, lady, she's here to get off heroin. Religion? Forget it.' I remember saying to Mum: 'When are you going to learn? If there was a God don't you think he would have answered your prayers by now?' She prayed constantly for me.

My parents went back to Canada, where they were living at the time, and I spent a year in this clinic. That was in 1983. At the clinic we were completely humiliated. You began to realise the despair and anguish that you caused other people, but they had a very strange way of doing things. One time I tried to leave and as a result I was dressed in blue overalls and nobody in the clinic spoke to me. There were about sixty people there. My place at the meal table was set upside down and I had to do things like clean the swimming pool with a tea cup and toothbrush. I couldn't understand how they thought that was going to get you off drugs: it seemed it was just to humiliate you.

Unfortunately it all took its toll on my mum. She had had cancer years before. With all the stress and trauma, it came back in a big way and I know my family felt that I wasn't making things any easier. As soon as I came out of the clinic I 'scored' again with heroin. It was because my mind was not healed: I had been in that clinic through force, and until you yourself decide that you want to do something it just doesn't work. Eventually, though, I did get myself back on my feet and I got good jobs and travelled quite a lot. I got the most fantastic job working in Vancouver. My mum was dying and it meant that I could go and live there with them. I had got the job off my own bat as well. I was beginning to feel quite good about myself.

I was with my mother when she died in 1987. She was really at peace when she went. She had an incredible faith. When she died one of the things she said to me was that I would never be happy without faith. She begged me to go to church, the Catholic church, but I thought she was off her rocker. Back in England I went on to get good jobs but something was still not quite right. Although I had great relationships with men, there was something missing. My oldest friend Daphne Stewart-Clark had 'got religion' about three or four years before that and she was always telling me to come to church and I would say, 'Daphne . . . forget it!' I could see that it had made a really, really huge difference to Daphne, which was great, but I said, 'It is not for me.'

Some time later, I phoned Daphne at nine o'clock one morning before I went to work. I had been out the night before with a load of people and had got absolutely drunk. It was awful because I suddenly found the old feeling of oblivion coming back. I realised that I wasn't happy and I phoned up in tears and Daphne came straight round. She said, 'Come on, Mary. Let's pray.' So we did and I was in tears, and at that stage I would have gone for anything. She then said, 'Why don't you do this Alpha course?'

I went along to the church she suggested and hated it. So I told Daphne where she could put her Alpha course and she said, bless her, 'Well look, Mary, I'm going to be helping on a course at another church in April or May. Why don't you do it and then I'll be there?' So I said: 'Well. . . .' And she said: 'Oh please, please give it a try.' That was the Alpha course at Holy Trinity in April or May of 1993.

I went and when everybody started singing I got very emotional. I found a real warmth and sincerity among the people that I hadn't seen before. They really cared. As I listened to the talks, it all really began to fall into place. Mark and Tamsin Carter, my group hosts, are now two of my closest friends. In the first group, Mark said, 'What would you like to pray for? Let's all pray for something and we'll see what happens during the course.' I was quite selfish and I thought, 'Well, all right. I need some real black and white signs here.' I said I wanted to pray for more gallery sales (I was working in a sculpture gallery) because things were absolutely dead. He said: 'All right, that's fine. Anything else?' And I said – I was being a bit flippant – 'Pray that I come back next week maybe.'

The following week I sold £85,000 worth of sculpture which I thought was a coincidence, but I went back because I felt that I had to go back and tell them.

I went back each week to Alpha, and soon it was time for the weekend away on the subject of the Holy Spirit. I didn't know whether I actually wanted to spend the weekend with a bunch of Christians. As it turned out, it was a very, very powerful weekend for me. Minutes into the first talk I was in floods of tears, and started shaking and sobbing. It was a very powerful feeling, but it was really safe. I can't compare it to anything I'd ever experienced before. I was so used to myself being dishonest that I would expect other people to be the same but it was wonderful and there was no doubt that God started working in my life.

On the Sunday morning James Odgers, who was leading the weekend, asked the Holy Spirit to come, and said: 'All those of you who want to ask Jesus Christ into your lives can say this prayer,' and he said a short prayer. I said it, and I *really* said it. I asked God into my life and I asked him to sort me out. That really did happen. He came into my life but I still felt unworthy. It wasn't until a Sunday service later on that I actually felt that I had been forgiven. People saw me in tears and it didn't matter because I knew I was safe to cry in front of those people. I am completely cleansed and God has given me the most fantastic sign of his love.

I recently moved to a flat in North Kensington and soon afterwards I was on my way home when I saw a woman who had dropped her shopping. I helped her pick it up and as I looked up I saw a sign which said 'Catholic Children's Adoption Society'. It is right at the end of my road. I called my father and said, 'Dad, did you get me from the Catholic Children's Adoption Society in St Charles' Square?' He said, 'Yes, that's right.' After that, I went round and round on my moped looking at it and I thought, 'God really has wiped my slate clean. He's brought me back to start my life again from where I started it.' I felt God saying: 'Thirty-something years ago you started your life here. You went off down the wrong road and now I'm giving it back to you.' He has given it back to me and I've given my life back to him now. It's so true when the Bible says how God 'restores the years the locust has eaten'.

There were some people I hurt where I might never be able to make amends: one of those is my mum . . . I'm sure she's doing somersaults up there now. For once I am so content. I had never cried before, but at church I have cried a lot. The point is that there's always somebody there. Even if I'm at home alone and I'm crying, I know I'm not alone any more because God is there. That is a real comfort. I remember thinking the other night how I always used to have my fix on my bedside table and I'd have a fix before I went to bed at night and then get it ready to have first thing in the morning. Now I've replaced that with my Bible. And I'm more passionate about the Bible than I ever was about my heroin. Indeed, my passion for heroin has been replaced by a far greater passion for Jesus Christ.

7

Pastoral Care

The first words of Jesus to Peter (in Mark's Gospel) were: 'Come, follow me . . . and I will make you fishers of men and women' (Mark 1:17). In his last conversation with Peter (in John's Gospel) Jesus repeated, 'Follow me!' (John 21:19) and urged Peter to feed and take care of the sheep and the lambs. The first priority is our relationship with Jesus. The second is our relationship with others.

In this last recorded conversation with Jesus on earth, Peter tells Jesus three times that he loves him. Each time Jesus' response is to tell Peter to look after other people. If we love Jesus, we will make this a high priority in our lives. Indeed it is part of following Jesus' example. He had compassion on people and once compared his longing to care for them and look after them to a hen with her chicks (Luke 13:34).

King David was a man who had experience of pastoral care as a shepherd tending sheep and also in the sense of being a shepherd of God's people. The psalmist says that 'David shepherded them with integrity of heart; with skilful hands he led them' (Psalm 78:72). Pastoral care involves our *hearts* and our *hands*. We must have an integrity of heart: our love for people and our friendship with them must be genuine. There must be no false pretence. This love needs to be combined with 'skilful hands'. There are skills which we can learn. Obviously in a short chapter we cannot look at all the skills of pastoral care but I want to mention some of the general principles involved in this area.

The apostle Paul wrote: 'We proclaim him, admonishing and teaching everyone with all wisdom, so that we may present everyone perfect in Christ. To this end I labour, struggling with all his energy, which so powerfully works in me' (Colossians 1:28–29).

Aims

Paul's aim was to 'present everyone perfect in Christ' (v 28). Some versions translate the word for perfect as 'mature'. Perfection is not something we can reach in this life, but it is possible to become mature. Three vital points emerge from this verse.

First, Paul's concern is for *everyone*. A good pastor will not want to lose any of his sheep. The aim on Alpha is that every single person should be looked after, which is why each group has two main hosts and two helpers. The idea is that one of the hosts or helpers should take responsibility for each of the members in the group. It is a flexible and very relaxed system but the clear aim is that everyone on the course should receive care and prayer.

This system of one-to-one care is perhaps the most crucial aspect of Alpha. For myself, I owe so much to the man who helped me on an individual basis, early on in my Christian life. He sacrificed his time to answer my questions, explain the Christian faith to me and to give me advice, guidance and friendship. It was always fun to be with him: indeed, it was the highlight of my week as he helped me to lay the foundations of my Christian life.

Care like this is much more likely to meet people's needs. Preaching and teaching are inevitably like throwing a bucket of water over empty bottles, whereas one-to-one pastoral care is like filling each bottle individually from the tap. Not only is it the most effective method, it is also a form of Christian service in which everyone can take part as it does not require great speaking or leadership gifts.

Juan Carlos Ortiz tells the story of meeting an old lady in his native Argentina, who introduced him to a young girl who was one of her great-grandchildren. She went on to tell him that she had six children and thirty-six grandchildren. Her family was impressive in number and among her grandchildren were many well-educated and professional people. Ortiz asked her, 'How did you manage to produce such a large, well-fed, well-dressed, well-educated, extended family?' She replied, 'I didn't. I just took care of the six and each of them took care of their six.'[24]

Preachers can overestimate the amount of truth that is assimilated between the pulpit and the pew. Bill Hybels and Don Cousins, leaders of the 17,000-strong Willow Creek Community church near Chicago, have spoken about their experiences of coming to realise that sermons in and of themselves do not prepare people to live effective Christian lives. Hybels states that every major strategic step or decision he has made was inspired and encouraged by someone three feet from him and not in a crowd of a thousand people. 'Truth applied across a table' has been a key to his own personal growth.

Secondly, our aim in this one-to-one pastoral care is *spiritual maturity*. Of course, this cannot happen overnight or even during a ten-week course. The hosts' and helpers' aim is to assist people through the early stages and then integrate them into a group within the life of the church, where they can grow and mature further.

The groups on Alpha are arranged, right from the start, with this express aim. That is why, ideally, the team in each small group should come from the same home group and at least one of the hosts or helpers should go with the group back to that home group and help introduce and integrate the new members.

Thirdly, Paul's aim is maturity *in Christ*. We do not want to attach people to ourselves but to Christ. Good parents encourage independence in their children. They begin by feeding their children but teach them, as soon as possible, to feed themselves. We need to beware of any unhealthy dependence on us and help people to become dependent on Christ.

Our aim is that every person who comes to Alpha should come to spiritual maturity in Christ. In practice, of course, a number of people do drop out, as we saw in Chapter 5. But as in the parable of the sower, those for whom the seed falls on good soil, 'hear the word, accept it, and produce a crop – thirty, sixty or even a hundred times what was sown' (Mark 4:20).

METHOD

Paul's method was to proclaim Christ. He wrote, 'We proclaim *him*, admonishing and teaching everyone with all wisdom' (Colossians 1:28). Jesus Christ is the key to spiritual maturity. We grow in maturity as our knowledge of him and intimacy with him grow.

Many of those who come on Alpha are not yet Christians. The

aim is to lead them to Christ. They may give their lives to Christ during one of the main sessions or they may do it on their own. But every host and helper should know how to lead someone into a relationship with Christ. *Why Jesus?* is the booklet we use on Alpha as a resource in this area. I use it myself when explaining the Christian faith to those who are not Christians and then I encourage them to pray the prayer in the back of the booklet. Sometimes they will want to pray it on their own, but more often they would prefer to pray it out loud with someone.

Once people have come to Christ, it is vital to encourage them to grow in that relationship. Bible reading and prayer are the keys to this. We need to help them with reading the Bible and advise them as to how they might pray on their own. We can give practical advice about which translation of the Bible might be appropriate to buy and guide them towards some suitable Bible reading notes. And it is good to explain that Bible reading is not an end in itself but a means of experiencing a relationship with Jesus Christ (John 5:39–40).

As well as the Bible, Christian books can be a great help. We encourage people to read a balanced diet of doctrinal, biographical and devotional books. Some are not great readers and prefer to listen to CDs of the Alpha talks and other subjects. We find many people enjoy listening to them in the car or when working around the home and this reinforces their faith.

In order to become mature in Christ, people need to grow in their relationships within the body of Christ. The small group is the ideal place to start developing such friendships. As weekly meetings proceed, friendships grow quite naturally. We can encourage the process by acting as a catalyst for discussion in the early stages, when people don't know each other well. Later, if they start coming to church, it can help if group members arrange to meet and sit together. If any of them live near each other, giving lifts encourages both the person who is giving the lift and the person who is receiving it, to come regularly.

ATTITUDE

In helping people on Alpha to grow into maturity in Christ, we have found three principles to be of great importance:

Encouragement

In his early Christian life, Paul was much encouraged by Barnabas. He in turn became a great encourager (Acts 16:40; 20:1–2). He also wrote urging Christians to 'encourage one another and build each other up' (1 Thessalonians 5:11). In the world there is so much negative criticism, leading all too often to insecurity and timidity. People shrivel up emotionally in an atmosphere of criticism and they thrive in an atmosphere of love and encouragement. We need to express warmth and responsiveness to those who are searching or are new Christians.

Listening

James writes, 'Everyone should be quick to listen, slow to speak. . .' (James 1:19). It is the task of the team on Alpha to draw out the guests and listen to them. We should take a genuine interest in them and encourage them to speak about themselves. If guests have ideas which are contrary to the Christian faith, we should not be quick to correct them. First, we need to listen, to try to understand where the other person is coming from and to show respect for people even if we disagree totally with their ideas. If they reach a point where they are interested and intrigued enough to ask us what we think, they will pay far more attention to what we have to say.

Peacemaking

Jesus said, 'Blessed are the peacemakers' (Matthew 5:9). It is important for the team on Alpha to be gracious and courteous and to avoid getting involved in arguments. On the whole, people will not be convinced if they get involved in an argument, especially if it is in front of others in the group. They tend to dig in their heels, which makes it harder for them to give up their position later if they wish to do so. It is easy to win an argument and lose a person. If there is an argument brewing, the host should try to reconcile differences and relieve tension, diplomatically exploring reasons

"...But the Hebrew for love is..."

for the differences. Usually there will be an element of truth in both points of view and the host can say, 'Isn't it a bit of both? Fred is right in saying . . . and George is right in saying. . . .' Then both Fred and George feel affirmed and the argument is over. Obviously, truth is what matters but the truth needs to be spoken in love and we need to be careful that 'speaking the truth' is not an excuse for a personality clash, an expression of anger, or a wrong exertion of authority.

COMMITMENT

Paul says, 'To this end I labour, struggling with all his energy, which so powerfully works in me' (Colossians 1:29). In Paul's pastoral care there was a balance between God's grace and his own responsibility. Our pastoral care should express the same balance. There is an element of 'toiling' and 'striving' involved in all effective Christian ministry.

Being on the team on Alpha involves a great deal of hard work. It requires a high level of commitment. Guests on Alpha are unlikely to reach a higher level of commitment than that of the hosts and helpers in their group. If the team does not attend regularly, those on Alpha are unlikely to do so. I ask hosts and helpers to rule out of their diaries all the evenings of the training course, as well as the ten Wednesdays of the course, the supper at the end and the weekend. Of course, occasions will arise when they are unable to attend, because they are abroad or required to work, or ill. But I ask them to give it the same priority they would give to their job.

This commitment is necessary because there are times when it will be a real effort to get there and talk to people sometimes until quite late at night. It requires an effort to talk to new people, rather than talking to friends. I ask people to pray and prepare beforehand so that when they are there they can concentrate all their efforts on the guests. This kind of effort makes for a very long evening.

Most important of all, helping on Alpha involves a commitment to pray. We ask the team to come to the prayer meeting at 6.15 pm every Wednesday, if they can possibly get away from work by then. We also ask them to commit themselves to praying regularly for every aspect of Alpha: the worship, talks, ministry and administration, as well as praying daily, if they can, for the individual members of their group.

The other side of our responsibility is God's grace. We do not 'labour' and 'struggle' on our own. We do it 'with all his energy, which so powerfully works' in us (Colossians 1:29). We need his help and his power for every task. When the disciples chose people to wait on tables they chose those who were 'full of the Spirit and wisdom' (Acts 6:3).

I encourage all the team to receive from the Lord, both at the prayer meeting beforehand and during the main session, as they enter into the worship and listen to the talk. Even if they have heard the talk several times before they can pray that God will show them something new and relevant to their lives. All the time I encourage them to pray for God to fill them with his Spirit and empower them with all the gifts they need: evangelism, teaching, pastoring and prophecy (the ability to hear what God is saying in a specific situation and pass it on to others).

It is this individual one-to-one pastoral care which is one of the most exciting aspects of Alpha. Members of the team often tell me thrilling stories about what has happened to an individual during the course. Not only has that individual's life been changed but it has brought great blessing to the member of the team who befriended him or her. There is no greater joy than to lead someone to Christ and watch them begin to grow in the faith.

The nineteenth-century evangelist R. A. Torrey, writing on the subject of pastoral care, said he believed that when the membership of any local church exercises its responsibility and privilege in this matter, and each and every member of church acts it out in the power of the Holy Spirit, 'a great revival will be close at hand for the community in which that local church is located. [It] is a work that wins but little applause from men, but it accomplishes great things for God.'[25]

The story of
Lee Duckett

8

Lee Duckett

When telecommunications engineer Lee Duckett came to do a job at Holy Trinity Brompton one morning, he didn't realise that it was a visit which would change his life. After years of depression, he had asked God to reveal himself to him – and God did exactly that. Here Lee tells what happened.

I learned a little about Christianity at primary school. In assembly once a week they did an Old Testament or a New Testament story and they got the kids up to act it. But I just took it as something for kids. When I was about eighteen years old, I started reading fantasy books and they influenced me quite a bit. I used to read a lot of books involving magic, gods, Arthurian history and also a lot of occult and New Age books. I considered myself an atheist although if I had to believe in some form of deity then I had more sympathy towards polytheism, as in the Norse or Greek gods, as I had read that they had been around longer.

I got involved with the occult after splitting up with my first girlfriend. We had been together four years, had got engaged, bought a flat and lived together for two years. After splitting I was heartbroken and we had to live in the same flat for six months as we had a negative equity mortgage. We saw each other on and off, in between her boyfriends, for another year and a half. Then she asked if we could get back together. It lasted for about a month. Two weeks later she told me she was getting married to someone else.

I fell into a state of depression. I was trying to get over her and so started searching for things to do. I went to see a medium a couple of times, tried out a ouija board quite a few times and dabbled in magic. After a couple of frightening experiences I stopped the magic. All the time the depression was getting worse; I was starting to close in on myself and couldn't bear to be near people. I also had a lot of thoughts about suicide. I started a course of hypnotherapy and psychoanalysis which lasted about three months consisting of weekly sessions. This was extremely hard work but after the complete treatment I felt really good for about a month. Then the depression started coming back.

I had a couple of strange experiences when I tried praying to God. One was when I was in the bath and I started crying. For some reason I said a prayer, saying that I believed God was real and accepted him. I said, 'Well, if you're there let me know.'

A few weeks later, in the course of my work, I came to Holy Trinity Brompton. I turned up at about 9.30 am and for me it was just another job. I did the work I had to do – which was putting in a new Mercury Smart Box – and then started chatting to the girl at reception. I'd been thinking about buying a Bible and I thought I would just read it as a story. So I was talking to Perry [a staff member] at reception (and thought she was nice and everything, you know!) when I said, 'What's a good Bible to buy?'

She thought the NIV was probably a good one and then said,

'We do this course. Would you like to go on it?' At first I thought I wouldn't but we got chatting and she was really nice. I asked her if she went to church and she said, 'Yes, I go and I'm a Christian. My friends and I are Christians and we have a lot of fun.' I couldn't understand what she meant at the time. I couldn't see how being a Christian was fun. She asked me again if I would like to do the course and I said, 'OK then.'

Being an engineer, I've always been the type that reads the instructions on things first. I like to know what I'm doing. I like to do something in a set sequence. As Perry explained what the course was, I thought, 'At least you've got someone to teach you.' I like being taught things. I like finding things out, but why make it hard for yourself? I like things to be easy and I find it easier if someone's teaching me.

I was going to be away on holiday when the next course came up, so Perry booked me up for six months later in September. She then gave me a copy of the booklet *Why Jesus?* which I read later. I said the prayer at the end of it but nothing dramatic seemed to happen.

I found myself looking forward to the Alpha course and on the first night I arrived early and sat in my car in the car park for half an hour. I saw all these people going into the church and thought that there was some kind of function on. I thought, 'It's a bit late for a wedding. I wonder what's going on in there?' I was only expecting there to be about thirty people and so was duly shocked when I was taken into the church to see 300 people who looked normal. I couldn't believe it. It certainly wasn't what I expected. I thought they would be people who would speak strangely and wear pairs of glasses with little bandages on – anorak jobs and stamp collectors. I was really amazed by how young the people were and there were some really nice women!

My team hosts were Ashley and Sibs Meaney and I just couldn't believe how at peace Ashley seemed to be. I thought, 'He's got what I'm missing. He's got something I want.' When we started to sing I felt really uncomfortable as though I were back at primary school. But I really enjoyed the talk and the group discussion afterwards and felt really good going home that night.

The next morning I woke up and started to have a wash and a shave. Then I looked in the mirror and this massive grin just came across my face and I started laughing. I was skipping around the house, laughing. I didn't know why. I just felt so happy. It was the first time I had smiled, *really* smiled, for about three years. I think with smiles you can tell by the eyes. With customers, I always put on this grin, but it wasn't a smile. My eyes were dead. But this time I smiled with my eyes too.

I bought an NIV Bible that Saturday and started at Matthew. I also started reading *Run Baby Run* by Nicky Cruz. Ashley invited me to church after the second Alpha evening and I felt really honoured to be invited. During that Sunday I spoke to Ashley about myself and my depression. That night the talk at the service was about depression. I stood up for ministry at the end and was prayed for by Ashley and his dad Baz. I felt their hands get really warm and I burst into tears and then felt a warm sensation rushing from my feet upwards, blowing the depression away.

During the following week I thought I was a Christian and tried telling some friends and family, but it was in an apologetic manner. Then over the next few weeks I started to become more at ease and was reading the Bible before going to sleep every night, reading Christian books and going to church on Sundays. One night, soon afterwards, I was in bed and after reading the Bible I started praying for the Holy Spirit to baptise me. I had been praying for about ten minutes and I felt as though there was a battle going on over me. All of a sudden I started thinking, 'Yea though I walk through the valley of the shadow of death I will fear no evil,' and I kept repeating this in my mind. I was really frightened. I then picked up my Bible and everywhere I opened it there were messages of the Lord's love and protection.

The next night I felt really uneasy in my bedroom and didn't sleep very well. The following day I phoned Ashley and told him about what happened. He said that he had been wondering when the Enemy would show up. He told me to get rid of the occult books and pictures in my room and to read Psalm 23 and Ephesians 6. The room did feel better after I had removed a picture and thrown some books away. That Wednesday the topic at Alpha was on evil. I had never felt so uncomfortable in church. I wanted to run. I felt nauseous and angry and wanted to leave immediately, but I did stay.

Then came the Alpha weekend, which was unbelievable. It felt as though we were developing real fellowship among the group and getting closer to the Spirit of God all the time. Nicky asked the Holy Spirit to come and fill us while we were all standing up. He said, 'He's working around the room,' and I heard and felt a blowing in my left ear. About two minutes later my knees started to buckle and I collapsed into my chair. I received the gift of tongues and at the end of the weekend I was full of joy and love for everyone.

We went to church that night and I was in the front row. I felt the presence of the Spirit all through the service. After the sermon we started to sing a song and I immediately felt God's presence and started to cry. Sandy [Millar, former Vicar of Holy Trinity] asked people to come forward for physical healing and I went forward for healing on my back. Sandy then asked the new Alpha people to help heal. A man called Ray came up to me and asked me what I wanted healing for. I said, 'My back,' and he asked if there was anything else, as my eyes were red from crying. I said 'No'. A husband and wife named Mike and Di from the Alpha task force came to help. I was taken to the side chapel and they started to pray for me. I felt the Spirit start from my feet and 'wash' through my body. I then felt the most unbelievably complete joy and began laughing uncontrollably. When it was all over I felt completely reborn. When I reached home I prayed in tongues in the car for half an hour and slept like a log that night.

On the Monday evening I phoned around all my friends really excited and told them about the weekend and that I had become a Christian. This time I wasn't apologetic! My life has completely changed. I now look at this world through different eyes. I feel love for everyone and an inner peace that I never imagined could exist. Now when I meet people I want to tell them about Jesus and whenever I hear of people like the IRA, although I sometimes think, 'Scum,' 95 per cent of the time I feel sorry for them and think, 'If only they knew Jesus like I am learning to know him.' I am also reading a lot of Christian books and I pray a lot in the car while driving.

My mum came to the Alpha supper. For Christmas she bought me a cross and chain which I didn't ask for. So I was really choked up about that because it shows she knows it means a lot to me. My mum and dad are just really pleased. All the family are. They take the mickey a bit. In fact they take the mickey a lot. But I keep inviting them to come. I feel the Spirit's presence almost every day. I obviously have many unanswered questions but just knowing God is enough.

9

Hosting Small Groups

John, a TV executive in his thirties, came with his wife, Tania, to an Alpha supper at the end of a course. Tania decided she wanted to do the next course, but John agreed to come along only reluctantly. He played little part in the discussion groups, apart from the occasional, rather negative, remark. On the weekend away he walked out of one of the sessions and told his wife they were leaving. She had become a Christian during the weekend and so was very disappointed. Nevertheless, she agreed to go with him. He told her on the way home that he was going to give up going to Alpha. I had not been involved in the weekend but Tania told me on Sunday of John's decision. So on the following Wednesday I was amazed to see him walk through the door. Later in the evening, when we were in small groups, we went around the group, each person reporting on their experience of the weekend. When it came to John, he told us what had happened. Naturally, I asked him why he had come back. He replied simply, looking at the group, 'I missed you lot.'

In John's case it was the small group which kept him coming to Alpha. He later gave his life to Jesus Christ and he and his wife are now firmly involved in the church. This incident shows us the vital importance of the small group.

The overall purpose of the small group, along with the course as a whole, is to help to bring people into a relationship with Jesus Christ. Jesus himself said that where two or three are gathered in his name he is there also (Matthew 18:20). We have found that a group of about twelve (comprising two hosts, two helpers and approximately eight guests) is the ideal size. I do not think it is a coincidence that Jesus chose a group of twelve (Mark 3:13–19).

THE SIX AIMS OF THE SMALL GROUP

1. Discussion

The groups meet to discuss the talk and issues arising out of the talk. It is vital to give people the opportunity to respond to what they have heard and to ask questions. This is especially the case if the group is made up predominantly of those who are not yet Christians. Usually such groups are not ready to study the Bible. When we first ran Alpha courses, the groups always studied the Bible from the first week. I soon realised that this was leading to considerable frustration. When the questionnaires came back at the end of the course there were comments such as, 'I only really enjoyed our group when we were allowed to spend the whole time discussing the talk.' Another wrote, 'I would have liked more time discussing the talk and more freedom to diverge from the set Bible study.'

The practical details are very important. The chairs need to be arranged so that everyone is comfortable and can see one another. Light and ventilation need to be good. Everyone should have access to a modern translation of the Bible. A good host aims to keep the discussion to the set time. We aim to start at 9.00 pm and finish at 9.30 pm. I discourage hosts from going on as a whole group beyond this time, even if they are involved in a rip-roaring discussion. It is always possible to say, 'Let's continue this next week,' which will encourage people to return to continue the debate. If the groups go on too long, people may be put off from coming back, fearing another late night.

Some groups are ruined by one of two things. First, ineffective leadership, where the host is not properly prepared or allows one person in the group to do all the talking. Or secondly, by an over-dominant host who does all the talking instead of giving those on the course the freedom to speak and to say what is on their minds. The host needs to be flexible enough to allow the group to change the subject, but confident enough gently to cut short 'red herrings' that are frustrating the majority.

It is important to ask simple questions. If you feel that the group is not ready for Bible study but discussion is not flowing very easily, possible questions to start discussion are listed in Appendix I of the training manual. Two basic questions to ask are 'What do you think?' and 'What do you feel?'

Hosts need to be prepared to help bring out answers to the issues raised in the group. I have found that some questions come up time and time again. The book *Searching Issues*[26] looks at the seven issues most often raised on Alpha. I encourage the hosts and helpers to be familiar with this material as well as reading around each of the subjects in it.

A good host will always be an encourager. At the most basic level this means smiling at people and being and looking inter-ested in what each person has to say. Even if someone says something that is not correct, a good host will respond with a phrase like 'How interesting', or 'I have never heard that before', or 'It might mean that . . .', and will then bring in the rest of the group to try to reach the right conclusion.

2. To model Bible study

The second aim of the small group is to learn to study the Bible together and to grow in knowledge. As mentioned already, the host should encourage the group members to do most of the talking and must resist the temptation to give a sermon.

Even if a Bible study is planned, it is important to give an opportunity to ask questions arising from the talk and to deal with these first. Otherwise, members of the group may feel frustrated that the real questions on their hearts and minds are not being answered.

If the group is ready for Bible study, the host needs to prepare the passage carefully. He or she should read the passage in different versions and make sure they understand it. They should try and spot any difficult verses and look up the explanation in a commentary (in order to avoid wasting time in the groups).

In the group setting, explain where the passage comes in the Bible and give the page number if using the same version, so that no one is embarrassed by their lack of knowledge. Sometimes it may be appropriate for each person to read a verse (for example, if you are looking at one of the Psalms); this gets everyone involved. For some passages (eg the prodigal son) it is better for the whole passage to be read by one good reader. Reading aloud can be a harrowing experience for some and they must be able to decline easily.

Then it is helpful to give a short introduction. For example, when studying the story of the prodigal son, one might begin by saying, 'Obviously, the father represents God and the son represents us. Let us see what lessons we can draw from the passage.' The introduction must be very short, perhaps one sentence, giving the main theme of the passage. It is a good moment to explain any obvious difficulties or ambiguous words. Hosts should be particularly careful to avoid using Christian jargon which excludes the non-Christian and the new Christian.

Next, the host has to get everyone talking. It is a good idea to work out the questions carefully in advance, and they should be kept short and simple. Questions that are either too vague (eg 'What is the difference between verses 7 and 17?'), too easy (eg 'Who died for us?'), or too difficult will not help to start discussion. Good questions to ask are open-ended ones that cannot be answered 'Yes' or 'No' and which provoke discussion of the key verses of the passage. The three basic questions to ask about any passage are 'What does it say?', 'What does it mean?' and 'How does it apply to our lives?'

The aim is to bring everyone into the discussion. Contributions from the quieter members of the group should be especially welcomed. If one person has done a lot of talking, it is good to ask, 'What do other people think?' Hosts should aim to learn as well as teach, and should not force their own ideas on the group. Even if we are asked directly for our own view, it is better, if possible, at first to deflect the question. Nor should we answer our own questions: it is better to re-phrase them.

Hosts should try not to repeat other people's comments unless they need clarifying for the rest of the group. If we are asked questions that we cannot answer it is fatal to bluff. We need to admit we do not know all the answers. Such an admission is often a good thing, and we can always tackle the question afterwards, or say that we will make a note of it and bring the answer next week. Better still, someone in the group might like to look up the answer. This helps the learning process, both for guests and for hosts. It is important we do not give the impression that there are easy answers to complicated questions or that we are great experts.

The most important thing is to make the study practical, so that everyone can see how they should apply the principles, and how God can use the passage to change their lives. There is no need to study for too long – 30-45 minutes is plenty.

3. To learn to pray together

If the host wishes to open in prayer, it must be done sensitively. The host may pray or, better still, ask a member of the group to do so. However, it needs to be done very carefully. They need to be asked beforehand and it needs to be made clear to the rest of the group that this is the case. Otherwise, people will be afraid that next time they themselves may be asked to open in prayer. (I know of one or two people who stopped coming because they thought they might have to pray aloud.)

To avoid embarrassment, the host could suggest a simple prayer (eg 'Will you ask God to give us wisdom to understand this passage?'), or, having asked someone beforehand, say to the group, 'I have asked X to open in prayer.'

Later on in the course, it may be appropriate to end with prayer. As most people find praying out loud quite daunting in the initial stages, it is important to talk about these difficulties and then model a very simple prayer, like 'Father . . . (short sentence) . . . for Jesus' sake. Amen.' This will encourage others that they could do something similar. Long eloquent prayers may be impressive, but they discourage others from praying. If we provide a simple model I have found that virtually everyone in the group prays, sometimes even those who are not yet Christians.

For those who do take the step and pray their first, faltering prayer, it can be a momentous occasion, giving new confidence to their relationship with God. It is deeply moving to hear someone's first public prayer. It is usually completely uncluttered by jargon and obviously comes straight from the heart. It is good to make clear to people that we all benefit when they muster the courage to pray aloud, however briefly and simply.

4. To develop lasting relationships within the body of Christ

It has often been said, 'People come to church for many reasons, but they stay there for only one: that they make friends.' We have found that extraordinarily close friendships are made during the course of the ten weeks. Four years ago I had a small group of twelve people, none of whom were Christians at the start of the course, but by the end they had all come to faith in Christ. All are now in positions of Christian leadership and remain very close. Immediately after the course, one of them said that before it had begun he had felt his 'friends register' was full and was amazed to find that he had made so many lasting relationships.

The hosts and helpers need to get to know each person in the group well. It is important to learn their names on the first night. Sometimes we play a name game to make this easier. Each evening the group sits together for supper and the hosts and helpers act as hosts and facilitate the conversations. Sometimes the group will go to a pub at the end of the evening, if people are comfortable with that. Sometimes they will meet up during the week, either on a one-to-one basis or all going out together as a group.

5. To learn to minister to one another

One small group I was involved in recently started out full of questions, some of which were quite hostile. They all seemed so different that I began to wonder whether they would all get on together, let alone minister to one another in the power of the Holy Spirit. But by the end it was wonderful to see them all praying for each other, laying on hands and praying for healing.

6. To train others to host

Alpha has grown at such a rate that we continually need more hosts. It has grown from one small group to thirty-five small groups on the current course. Initially, the hosts were experienced Christians, often of at least ten years' standing. Many of the helpers these days have become Christians on the previous Alpha course and even the hosts may have been Christians for as little as six months. This is not ideal, but it is a good problem to have: presumably the early church was faced with a similar situation. When 3,000 were converted on the Day of Pentecost some of them must have needed to lead virtually straight away.

Paul tells Timothy to entrust the things he taught him 'to reliable people who will also be qualified to teach others' (2 Timothy 2:2). It has been said that 'Delegation without training leads to disappointment', and we make sure that all hosts and helpers have done the three-session Alpha Team Training Course. The helpers can learn more about leadership from watching the hosts of their group 'in action', and it is hoped that the hosts' model may one day be useful to all the group members.

The story of
Derek and Francie Lygo

10

Derek and Francie Lygo

When Derek and Francie Lygo's three-month-old daughter Chloe was a victim of cot death, their world fell apart. Here Francie, who went on to give birth to their second daughter Freya, tells the story of what happened and how a new-found relationship with God has changed both their lives.

I've always been brought up in the Christian tradition. Derek was an atheist but we were married in church. It was love at first sight, and we were engaged within two weeks of meeting each other. We still love each other, probably even more than we loved each other then, if that's possible.

Ever since I was a child, I have always felt that there would be a time in my life when I would get to know God better. I didn't know when that would be but I knew it would be sometime. I don't think thoughts like that had ever even occurred to Derek. Life when we were married was going very well: he had a very good job in the City and we were on the crest of a wave. It wasn't always easy but we were very, very happy.

Then I became pregnant with Chloe which was the fulfilment

of our dreams. We had wanted a baby as soon as we were married. We were thinking of moving into a bigger house and gearing up the mortgage. I did not have an easy pregnancy and I was very ill in hospital for about six weeks before her birth. But Chloe was born and she was a lovely bouncy, happy baby and everything was wonderful.

Nothing, nothing in the world could have prepared us for what was going to happen next. It was 26 November 1991, in the evening, that she stopped breathing. It was a moment of distraction: Derek was on the phone, I was cooking supper, and when I went to look at her a few minutes later, I found her dead. Derek called an ambulance and we attempted to revive her before it came. Eventually it arrived and she was raced to St George's Hospital, Tooting, where she was put in Intensive Care.

It was awful when they were trying to get her heart going. It took a long time, probably about forty-five minutes, and a human being dies in three minutes if they don't get oxygen. So that in itself was amazing, that after forty-five minutes they were able to start her heart beating again. She was put on a life support machine and never breathed on her own again. She lived another seventeen hours, and they were the longest hours in my life. A second seemed like a day, a minute seemed like a year and an hour seemed like eternity. We didn't know what to do with ourselves. There are no words that can describe parents' feelings. She was our life. One minute we had a bouncy, healthy baby and the next minute the person our whole lives revolved around was dying. Our lives came to a grinding halt. We were unprepared and numb. We wanted to be with her, but the agony of seeing her was almost too much to bear. We were sick with shock and exhausted beyond belief. We had done everything for her in the past but now we found ourselves helpless and other people had taken over. We could not just pick our baby up, walk out of that place and give her a cuddle which we longed to do. Everything was alien to us and it was a struggle to take it in.

But it was in this situation that the Lord showed his compassion, which was amazing. I had always wanted Chloe baptised. Before she became ill Derek was indifferent to it and he hadn't wanted a big fuss but now he agreed and we decided she had to be baptised. Gradually it became obvious that we were going to lose her and as our hopes for her life faded we realised it was an ordeal we would have to live through. The chaplain was there and we had her baptised. Moments after the baptism I said to Derek, 'The Holy Spirit's here!' and I didn't know anything about the Holy Spirit. God's love for me was so incredible that he sent his Spirit down to comfort me at that time. I felt this amazing source of strength and peace.

Towards the end our nurse said she thought I should hold Chloe. I was frightened I'd hurt her. Then she said, 'I think she'd far rather be in your arms.' So I took her and she died in my arms. But before that happened, I felt God. I felt overwhelmed with his love and I felt held in his arms, as I was holding Chloe in mine. And the extraordinary thing is that I didn't really know that any of these things could happen. I wasn't a proper Christian at all, apart from going through the traditional motions, and yet that's when I knew that I'd had a physical experience of his love and light. There were tears, but no hysteria. The calmness came from him. I felt I had no right to hold her back and though my heart was breaking as I held her little hand I knew with certainty she was with

Jesus and that Jesus himself had been longing to hold and care for her.

Then we left the hospital and we came home and we had no child. I was thrown into a pit of despair and my world was black: it was like I was suspended in a well of black ink. All around there was suffocating blackness; I couldn't look out of a window and feel joy, as part of me had died. Nothing could lift me, I was so, so sad.

We went to Florida for Christmas as had been planned. When we came back, I bumped into Susie Farley, a neighbour I had met at ante-natal classes. Of course I had no baby, and her little baby Harry was there and she asked where Chloe was, and I had to tell her. She was so kind. She was obviously very sad and asked me if I was a Christian. My words to her were that I didn't know if I was, if God could allow such things, yet all the time I knew I'd experienced his love. Susie asked me if I'd think of going to Alpha, a course at her church, Holy Trinity Brompton. I wouldn't have gone if she hadn't driven me there and introduced me to others. But the wonderful thing was that the moment my feet walked over the threshold of the room there, I felt the same feeling of light and joy and love that I'd known at the time of Chloe's death.

I never looked back after that moment. That was the only thing that lifted me. I went back again and completed the course. People were so kind. I suddenly knew there was the sky and there were birds in it and there was a rainbow and wonderful things around. There was something worth living for again. Derek couldn't believe the difference in me. He was very suspicious because he thought I was getting involved in some Moonie religious organisation and he thought he had to stamp it out, fast. I managed to persuade him to come on the next evening Alpha course. Very sweetly he said he'd come for me. For the first five weeks he was aggressive and used convincing arguments against becoming a Christian.

Then one day, halfway through the course, he was sitting in the barber's shop and looking at himself, and he prayed that God would come into his life. He now says that God answered immediately and that he felt the whole of the heavens rejoice as though a voice was saying, 'At long last! We've been waiting all your life for you to do this. Thank you for doing it!'

Our lives changed dramatically after that point. Derek resigned from his job, so we had almost a year together while he was unemployed. The Bible talks about putting us in a spacious place (eg Psalm 18:19) and God did. He gave us the space we needed to be ourselves and to build our faith. He has more than provided for us in every possible way. He has given us wonderful friends – far closer than we've ever had before – who pray for all parts of our lives consistently. In the same week that our second child, Freya, was born, Derek got the job he's in now which is just right for him. It was such a clear demonstration of God's perfect timing for our lives.

Every day I cry for Chloe. I still love her. Some months after she died I did ask the question 'Why?' because she seemed so perfect and it seemed such a waste. You always know when it's God replying because the answer is so powerful. I sensed him say, 'Chloe is much happier in heaven than she would ever have been on earth.' And I said, 'But I loved her so much, Lord. There was so much that I wanted to teach her, so much I wanted to show her.' He said to me, 'Now do you understand why you need to love me at least as much as you love Chloe? There is so much I want to teach and show you.'

Little Freya is the most lovely child and we delight in her. As Freya grows up we see how much she would have loved to have had a sister. She adores other children. Grief is not something you 'get over' like a bad cold, and the pain is something you learn to live with; it's the physical absence of the person you love which is the hardest thing to bear. But the Lord continues to be our strength. He has never yet failed us. He continues in his Spirit to heal and comfort us and we always arrive at a restored peacefulness once more. There is no secret to knowing his love. We only have to seek it. Through Chloe's death I knew what 'it' was all about and that in suffering I was growing up, literally overnight. Growing up is learning to accept God's will (sometimes it's hard to grow up). This for me was the moment of reckoning. I felt I had only half-lived. My spirit has been awakened and this was an aspect to my existing on this earth which I had never known before.

The Lord must not only have loved me beyond my understanding but I think he knew that once I knew and loved him, I would never turn back from his power on my life and my family. It has been too strong a force. I will never forget his goodness to me in my darkest hours. I was nothing before him and I would be nothing without him – he is the centre of my life.

11

Giving Talks

Before I was a Christian, I was dragged to a talk which was one of a series in a mission at Cambridge. I remember looking at the clock at the start, determined not to listen and watching it all the way through the talk, amazed at how long it went on and how bored I was. Others seemed to be enjoying it and laughing. But I had told myself that I would not listen to a word of it.

When speaking to Christians it is not unreasonable to assume an interest. We expect from the congregation a hunger to find out more about the Christian faith, to try to understand doctrine and study the Bible. With those who are not Christians we cannot make any such assumptions. Rather it is wise to assume they are asking, 'Why should I listen?' and are challenging us to say something of interest to them.

We need to respond to this challenge. In the opening words, we have to tell them why they should listen. Truth in itself is not necessarily of interest. Truth is not the same as relevance. If we start by saying, 'I want to expound the doctrine of justification by faith,' then they are likely to fall asleep. On the whole, people are not interested in theology or historical background until they see its relevance. We must arouse their interest right at the beginning: the first few seconds are vital.

They have got to think, 'This is interesting. . . .' Like Jesus we need to begin with a need, a hurt, or something else of interest to the audience. Humour may be a way in, providing it leads us on to what we want to say. On the whole, people will listen to stories, whether they are humorous or serious. These should then lead into a subject of relevance to the hearers: work, stress, loneliness, relationships, marriage, family life, suffering, death, guilt, or fear.

In this chapter I want to look at the whole subject of speaking to non-churchgoers (eg those on Alpha) and in particular at giving an evangelistic talk (eg the Alpha supper at the end of the course). I believe it is a skill which many people could acquire. The major requirement is a strong desire to communicate the good news about Jesus Christ. In preparing such a talk there are seven vital questions we need to ask. We will look at each of these in turn.

IS IT BIBLICAL?

The Bishop of Wakefield, the Rt Revd Nigel McCulloch, described a sermon, which he heard while he was on holiday, as a 'disgrace'. 'The preacher spoke long, but said little. There was no message. As I looked around at my fellow-worshippers I could see from the sleeping of the old and the fidgeting of the young that they, like me, were finding the sermon dull, uninspiring and irrelevant. What a lost opportunity. In fact, what a disgrace.' He did not reveal the content of the sermon, but he did observe that 'the congregation does not want third-rate personal comments on public affairs but real preaching that brings the Bible to life. . . . If St. Paul had been asked to advise the Church of England what to do in the Decade of Evangelism he would tell us what he told Timothy. In every pulpit, in every church, at every service "preach the word".'[27] This does not mean that talks to people who don't go to church must necessarily be biblical exposition. Rather they should be based on biblical truth and have verses of the Bible weaved into their fabric.

In giving an evangelistic talk at the Alpha supper at the end of the course there are certain ingredients that I always try to include. Paul said that when he went to Corinth he 'resolved to know nothing . . . except Jesus Christ and him crucified' (1 Corinthians 2:2). I try to ensure that every such talk is centred on Jesus. First, I say something about who he is, that Christianity is a historical faith based on the life, death and resurrection of Jesus Christ, that the same Jesus is alive today and that it is possible for us to have a relationship with him. Secondly, I include something on 'him crucified'. I speak of what Jesus did on the cross when he died for us and how he made it possible for our sins to be forgiven and our guilt to be removed. Thirdly, I explain how someone can enter into a relationship with God, referring to repentance, faith, and receiving the Holy Spirit.

IS IT GOOD NEWS?

In his first sermon, Jesus chose to preach on the text from the prophet Isaiah, 'The Spirit of the Lord is on me, because he has anointed me to preach good news to the poor' (Luke 4:18). Jesus did not come to condemn the world but to save it. The gospel is good news in a world which is full of bad news. We should not simply make people feel guilty. We may need to talk about sin and guilt. But we do not want to leave people there. We are telling them about Jesus who frees us from sin, guilt and evil. That is good news.

When Philip spoke to the Ethiopian eunuch he 'told him the good news about Jesus' (Acts 8:35). I explain in the talk at the Alpha supper that Jesus Christ meets our deepest needs. I know that those listening who are not yet Christians will be struggling somewhere deep down with a lack of ultimate meaning and purpose in their lives; they will have no satisfactory answer to the inevitable fact of death or the universal problem of guilt. In all probability they will also be aware of a sense of 'cosmic loneliness', a sense of being in God's world without the God for and by whom they were made.

Aware of these needs I try to show how Jesus dealt with our guilt on the cross, how he defeated death by his resurrection, how he made possible a relationship with God which gives meaning and purpose to life, and how he gives us his Holy Spirit so that we need never experience that cosmic loneliness. Of course, the good news of the kingdom of God includes far more than this. But in a twenty-minute talk at an Alpha supper I stick to a few very basic parts of this good news. Whenever I have finished writing a talk I ask myself the question, 'Is this talk good news?'

IS IT INTERESTING?

We live in an age of TV and computer games. People are not used to listening to long talks and it can be hard to retain their attention. Undiluted theology will not grip most people for very long. They prefer listening to stories and hearing how the point of them fits in with their lives. As a general rule, I find it helpful to follow the formula: point, illustration, application. If a talk has three points it will look something like this:

Introduction
(i)   Point
     – illustration
     – application
(ii) Point
     – illustration
     – application
(iii) Point
     – illustration
     – application
Conclusion

It is worthwhile collecting illustrations. They come primarily from our own experience, but they can also come from newspapers, radio, TV, films, plays, books and magazines. Of course, many of the best illustrations come from the Bible itself or from the natural world, and we need to think out carefully the applications for our listeners.

Is it persuasive?

Paul tried 'to persuade' people (2 Corinthians 5:11). We need to work out what we are trying to achieve in a particular talk. For instance, are we trying to lead people to Christ, persuade them to start reading the Bible, or to pray? It is worth writing down at the top of the talk what our aim is. If we aim at nothing we are likely to hit nothing. If we aim at too much our efforts are likely to be dissipated. C. H. Spurgeon, the nineteenth-century preacher, said, 'One tenpenny nail driven home and clenched will be more useful than a score of tin-tacks loosely fixed, to be pulled out again in an hour.'[28]

Having established the aim we need to ensure that every point is focused in that direction, like a tent supported from three or four different angles. We need to use every argument to appeal to the minds, hearts and wills of the hearers.

There must be an appeal to the mind. We must give people reasons for doing what we are urging them to do. Over the Alpha course we try to teach all the basic elements of the gospel. At an evangelistic Alpha supper we try to teach the crucial elements of the good news.

If the talk were only appealing to the mind, it would be very

162

dry. We need also to appeal to the heart. If, like me, you are British, you may find that hard. But people's emotions are involved as well. If it were purely an appeal to the emotions there would be a danger of emotionalism. Conversely, in appealing purely to the mind, we can stray into intellectualism.

Ultimately, if we are to persuade people to make a decision we need to appeal to their wills. In an evangelistic talk I try to drop a hint early on that there is a decision to be made, that there is no neutral ground, and there are no 'don't knows' in the kingdom of God. I let them know what the options are. They can refuse Christ or accept him or just put off the decision. All this must be done without any pressure. It is right to persuade but wrong to pressurise.

Is it personal?

Bishop Phillips Brooks defined preaching as 'the bringing of truth through personality'.[29] Of course, the message we want to get across is objectively true and much of what we say will be proclaiming that truth. However, it is a great help for the hearers if we can illustrate these truths from our own experience. We need to be honest and real, not pretending that we are perfect or that we never struggle in any areas of our lives. This does not mean that we have to make embarrassing public confessions, but it is a help to acknowledge our own difficulties and failures. Stories told against ourselves can be both amusing and encouraging at the same time, provided they are set in a context which builds faith and is not purely negative. For example, I often tell stories about my early attempts at evangelism and the ridiculous things I did. I do it partly as a joke against myself, but also to assure people that we all make mistakes.

It is wise to talk generally in terms of 'we' rather than 'you'. 'You' can be very threatening and it suggests that we are somehow putting ourselves above our hearers. 'We' is less threatening since it gives the impression that we are all in the same boat. 'I' is the least threatening since it does not intimate that the hearers have the same problems: if it is used too frequently, however, the talk will appear self-centred. Generally I would suggest that 'you' and 'I' should be used sparingly. 'You' is often effective at the end of a talk: 'What do *you* make of the claims of Christ?' 'Will you decide today . . .?'

IS IT UNDERSTANDABLE?

It is no use giving the greatest talk in the world if no one can understand it. It is often said that we should never overestimate an audience's knowledge and never underestimate their intelligence. Because knowledge is limited we need to avoid jargon (which is familiar only to the 'in' crowd) and technical terms such as 'justification', 'sanctification', 'holiness' and 'atonement' or any other word which is not used in everyday speech. The only case for using such words is if we explain simply what we mean by them.

The other side of the coin is that because most people's intelligence is reasonably high, there is very little that they will not understand provided it is clearly explained. Many theological books and talks are incomprehensible to most people: reasonably enough, if they are technical books for experts. However, I know for myself that if what I am saying gets very complicated, it is usually because I myself do not fully understand it. Albert Einstein once said, 'You don't really understand something unless you can say it in a really simple way.'

Certainly the teaching of Jesus was basically very simple. His economy in the Lord's Prayer, which comprises fifty-six words, is very favourable when compared to a recent EC regulation report on the sale of cabbages which totals 26,901 words!

IS IT PRACTICAL?

The Bible often exhorts us to be 'doers' rather than just 'hearers'. James writes, 'Do not merely listen to the word and so deceive yourselves. Do what it says' (James 1:22). Jesus himself said that what distinguished the wise man (who built his house upon a rock) from the foolish man (who built his house on sand) was that the wise man put into practice what he heard (Matthew 7:24), whereas the foolish man did not.

If we are to help people put into practice what they hear, then we need to be very practical. We need to show them how they can do what we are talking about. In an evangelistic talk we should explain carefully what a person needs to do if they want to give their life to Christ. The vital elements in the New Testament response seem to be repentance, faith, and receiving the Holy Spirit. I explain these using the words sorry, thank you and please.

I explain repentance in terms of asking forgiveness for the past and turning away from everything we know to be wrong (that is 'sorry'). I explain faith as putting our trust in what Jesus did for us on the cross ('thank you') and I explain receiving the Spirit in terms of asking him into our lives ('please'). Then I pray a prayer along the lines of the one in the booklet *Why Jesus?* and make it possible for them to pray that prayer in their hearts along with me.

165

Finally, it is good to remember that it is more important to prepare ourselves than to be prepared in the technique of giving talks. Billy Graham, speaking to 600 clergy in London in November 1979, said that if he had his ministry all over again he would make two changes. The audience looked rather startled. What could he mean? He said he would study three times as much as he had and he would give himself more to prayer. He quoted Dr Donald Gray Barnhouse who said, 'If I had only three years to serve the Lord, I would spend two of them studying and preparing.'

The story of Bernie Keane

12

Bernie Keane

London cab driver Bernie Keane had been a churchgoer – on and off – for much of his life when he heard about the Alpha course at Holy Trinity Brompton. He and his wife Pamela decided to attend the course in October 1996. Here he explains how his attitude to God and life in general has totally changed.

I was born in St Stephen's Hospital on the Fulham Road and was brought up in the Kensington and Chelsea area. When I was one year old, I got whooping cough, which led to spells in a children's hospital in my early years and left me with something called bronchiectasis. I was brought up in a strict Roman Catholic household. I became an altar boy at about nine years old. Later, I went to church on Sunday, but if I could get out of it, I would.

I left school at fifteen and became a carpenter. Then I decided I didn't want to do that and became a fishmonger in New King's Road. I packed that in because a girlfriend said, 'I like you, Bernie, but I don't like the smell of you.'

As a teenager in the sixties, I was a scooter boy. Every weekend we used to drive down to Brighton, stay down there for the weekend, sleep on the beach, get drunk, drive back. I was totally into myself, the girls and having a good time. I carried on until I was over thirty. I was drinking and clubbing – but to me I was having a good time. Later I managed a bookshop in the Cromwell Road, where I met my lovely wife Pamela, who was working in the shop next door.

I stopped going to church when I was a teenager. It wasn't until I met and married Pam that I took an interest in going to Mass and visiting her church in Scotland – Pamela is Scottish. This slowed me down to a proper pace of lifestyle.

My first experience of Christianity from a different perspective was when I met a Greek shipping magnate who had become a Christian. He invited me to go and hear a missionary in a church hall over in Southwark, where there were a lot of down-and-outs. It was a marvellous sermon and at the end of it he asked anybody who wanted to be saved to stand up. I stood, but I didn't really understand it. I always have fond memories of the chap because I feel that he planted the first seed of Christianity into me.

To be a London cabbie involves learning all the streets and prominent buildings in London. It takes two to three years if you are good and you work hard at it. I used to get on my bike and ride around London every afternoon and then I would go off to night school in the evening. Weekends would be spent 'calling over' with a friend – calling out all the streets parrot fashion. To start off, they give you 600 runs, which all zigzag across London. You have to learn these 600 runs, picking up streets and points along the way. It's like a jigsaw.

The first night I went to night school, I thought, 'This is impossible,' but your knowledge builds up – that's why they call it 'The

Knowledge'. I sat fourteen exams to be a cab driver. For every twelve people who start The Knowledge, eight pack it in. In 1985, I became a cab driver and I have done it ever since.

When my daughter, Laura, was born, she was baptised a Roman Catholic. I felt I had to give her some lead in faith. I started taking her to church. My wife used to come with me sometimes. We also attended my wife's church when we were in Scotland.

About ten years ago, we went to a Billy Graham event at Earl's Court and I was fascinated by it. At the end I went down to the front and went up to one of the counsellors who wore a badge. We started talking and it was amazing. Of all the thousands of people there, he had a daughter in the same school and the same class as my daughter. I had a nice chat to him and he said, 'Why don't you join a Bible class?'

I went to the Bible class he recommended but, looking back on it now, I wasn't ready then. I stopped.

I carried on going to the Catholic church with my daughter, sitting at the back. I was just going through the motions. The only bits of the service I used to enjoy were when they read the Gospel, gave the notices, and when we shook hands. The rest was a long drawn out ritual to me.

In the summer of 1996, Pamela and I went on holiday to Spain. We have some friends who have retired there. While there, they told us they had become Christians and they took us to a prayer meeting up in the mountains led – through a translator – by a couple of Colombian missionaries. These people had given up everything in Colombia and I was fascinated. At the end of the evening they invited people to come forward and be blessed. They put their hands on people and prayed for them.

Then the daughter of my friends said, 'Have a read of this psalm, Bernie. I always read this when I am a bit low or down and it gives me great strength.' It was Psalm 139 ('O Lord, you have searched me and you know me. You know when I sit and when I rise . . .'). I read it. It was wonderful. She said, 'Why don't you go and have the blessing?' I thought, 'I am up in the mountains. It is the nearest I am going to get to God!' So I went up and had a blessing. People prayed for me for quite a while.

I felt these people were very genuine and real – and very, very committed to God. I was interested in becoming part of them.

I started chatting to my friend afterwards and she said, 'When you go back, why don't you and Pam do the Alpha course?' I asked what it was all about. They gave me a copy of *Alpha News* and I read up a little bit about it. I came back and saw that there was one in Wimbledon and one in Richmond, where my wife works. Then I read that Nicky Gumbel did one at HTB. I thought, 'Let's go and see the top man. Let's go and do it with the top boy.' My wife said she could drive from Richmond and I was up in town with my cab anyway. It worked out fantastically. We started the course in October 1996.

On the first night I walked in and thought, 'Blimey!' I was expecting a little village hall atmosphere with about forty people. I never expected it to be 500 people. I sat down and had the food and thought that it was very nice, but I remember saying to myself, 'Oh my word, it's a bunch of middle classes having a cosy little chat about Jesus over a casserole.' I always finish things I start, though, and after a couple of weeks, I relaxed and started enjoying Nicky's talks and relating to them greatly. I was very pleased with the group I was in too.

After about three or four weeks I was really getting into it. My wife and I would go home at night and sit up until one o'clock chatting about it all. I found it very amusing that we were going to stay at Pontins for the weekend. The Holy Spirit has always been a big thing for me and I was looking forward to it.

On the Saturday, Nicky started talking about the Holy Spirit and I said, 'Lord, I am trying to be sincere. Please fill me with the Holy Spirit.' I have always felt spiritually very hollow. Nothing happened.

On the Sunday morning, I prayed again and suddenly felt a calmness over me. I felt a smile coming on my face. I felt so wonderful that there aren't any words to do it credit.

The only way I can describe it is that I got rid of all that guilt and all the hang-ups I had about religion. I just felt, for the first time in my life, that I had a relationship with God. I always wondered what people meant when they said, 'I have got a relationship with God,' but I felt then I had a relationship with God. My wife says she has noticed a big change in me.

I read my Bible every day now. I wouldn't have done that before. My wife has just bought me a big Bible for my fiftieth birthday. It has got a lot of references in it and I find it very helpful. I can't get enough of it. I have to stop myself reading it because my wife keeps reminding me that I have got other responsibilities, like going to work and doing a few jobs around the house!

I now have a relationship with Jesus. I can talk to him. Before I was always asking him for things, but I spend more time thanking him now. I thank him for what has happened during the day, what has happened in my life. He has strengthened my marriage.

My sister-in-law accuses me of joining the God Squad and the guys down at the pub say I have become the Tambourine Man – but they all want to know what is going on.

I now go to an evangelical church in the same road that I live in – Worple Road, Wimbledon. I was just amazed at the fellowship when I walked in there, just the friendliness of the people. I have since thought back to all those years of going to church. I was trying to get to know God, but didn't know how.

I keep *Why Jesus?* and an Alpha pamphlet in the cab and sometimes I say to passengers, 'Go along and try it. It doesn't cost you anything. It is like ten evenings out at the theatre! And you get a nice meal for £2.50.'

I think Alpha taught me how to have a relationship with God. I talk to God now. I get on my knees every day – I would never have done that before.

13

Ministry

What makes Alpha so exciting is the work of the Holy Spirit among us. It is his activity which transforms the talks, the discussion groups, the Bible studies, pastoral care, administration and every other aspect of Alpha. The word 'ministry' is used in several different ways in the New Testament and in the church today. In one sense, ministry includes everything done in a church and every aspect of an Alpha course. John Wimber defined ministry as 'meeting the needs of others on the basis of God's resources'. *The New Bible Dictionary* points out, 'In its earliest form the Christian ministry is charismatic, ie it is a spiritual gift or supernatural endowment, whose exercise witnesses to the presence of the Holy Spirit in the Church.'[30] In this chapter, however, I am using a narrower sense of the word: when we specifically pray for others in the power of the Holy Spirit.

One of the most astonishing stories in the Old Testament is the account of Moses and the people of Israel crossing the Red Sea. When they came to the sea God said to Moses, 'Raise your staff and stretch out your hand over the sea to divide the water so that the Israelites can go through the sea on dry ground' (Exodus 14:16). God was asking Moses to do his part while promising to do his own part, by dividing the sea. I wonder what went through Moses' mind at that moment. He would have felt an idiot if he had stretched out his hand and God had not divided the sea. He may have thought it would have been much easier if God had just divided the sea without involving him. But as is often the case in the Bible, there is a co-operation between us and God. God allows us to be involved in his plans. We do our part and God does his. Our part is relatively simple. God's is not so easy.

Moses took a step of faith and 'stretched out his hand' (Exodus 14:21). God responded and '. . . all that night the Lord drove the sea back with a strong east wind and turned it into dry land. The waters were divided, and the Israelites went through the sea on dry ground, with a wall of water on their right and on their left' (Exodus 14:21–22).

God has not changed. This story reminds us that when we do what he asks us to do, he does what he has promised to do. As we pray for others he sends his Holy Spirit to transform lives. This might be prayer for others to be filled with the Spirit, to receive some gift (eg the gift of tongues), or prayer for healing.

MINISTRY VALUES

The most fundamental thing here is to recognise that this is a ministry of the Holy Spirit. It is not our power but his. What God asked Moses to do was very simple; he did not have to shout or dance or leap about. Likewise, we encourage our hosts to be totally natural and simply to be themselves, to take a step of faith and stretch out their hands and ask God to send his Spirit. The rest is up to him. Sometimes I look around while ministry is happening and see hosts or helpers stepping out in faith for the first time in this area. There is often an expression of astonishment, bewilderment and joy on their faces as they see how God uses them.

Sometimes when we see the extraordinary work of the Spirit we may be tempted to look at the fruit rather than the vine. But we are to keep looking to Jesus. Jesus taught his disciples not to be sidetracked in any way from the most important issues. When the seventy-two returned joyfully from the places they had been sent to minister to and said, 'Lord, even the demons submit to us in your name' (Luke 10:17), Jesus replied, 'I saw Satan fall like lightning from heaven. I have given you authority to trample on snakes and scorpions and to overcome all the power of the enemy; nothing will harm you. However, do not rejoice that the spirits submit to you, but rejoice that your names are written in heaven' (Luke 10:18–20).

Secondly, and of equal importance, all ministry must take place under the authority of the Bible. The Spirit of God and the written word of God will never be in conflict. They complement each other. God will never do or say anything which is inconsistent with his revealed will and character in the Bible. Because the word and the Spirit go hand in hand we encourage our hosts to be steeped in the biblical truths and promises as part of ministry. It is the truth that sets people free (John 8:32). I ask people to make sure they know where key passages are that relate to the kinds of needs which emerge as we pray for people. For example, some of the passages we often use are the following: Psalm 51 (repentance), Psalm 91 (fear), Philippians 4:6–7 (anxiety), Psalm 37:5 (guidance), 1 Corinthians 10:13 (temptation).

Our third main concern in ministry is the dignity of the individual: if we love people we will show them respect. This means first that confidentiality is assured. If people tell us confidential matters about their lives they need to be assured it will go no further. It will not be 'shared for prayer' or discussed at helpers' meetings. Next, we must affirm rather than condemn. We don't say, 'It's your fault,' if people are not healed, or suggest that it was because they did not have enough faith. Jesus never told an individual that it was their lack of faith that stopped them being healed. Occasionally he upbraided his disciples for their lack of faith (and we may need to ask ourselves whether we lack faith) but he never condemned the sick person in this way. We should not place additional burdens on anyone, let alone those who are sick. If they are not healed we never suggest that they should believe that they are. Rather we give them the freedom to come back and pray again. This kind of prayer should always be done in a low-key way and any super-spirituality and unnatural intensity should be avoided at all costs.

The fourth value is harmonious relationships. Jesus prayed for his disciples, 'May they be brought to complete unity to let the world know that you sent me and have loved them even as you have loved me' (John 17:23). The unity of the people of God was a high priority on Jesus' agenda and it should be so on ours. A lack of unity, love and forgiveness on the team hinders the work of the Spirit and is a terrible example to those on Alpha. It is vital that each group's hosts and helpers find time to pray together, as prayer is the most effective way of rooting out petty irritations. We make it a rule on Alpha never to criticise another denomination, another Christian church or a Christian leader. We try to support and encourage one another constantly. I discourage anyone from making negative remarks about another team member even as a joke. We are extremely careful during the entertainment on the weekend away not to allow any skits which have even a hint of cynicism or are in any way negative. This may seem excessive, but we have found in the past that even the most off-the-cuff comment can have a detrimental effect.

Our fifth value is the vital importance of the body of Christ. The Christian community is the place where long-term healing and spiritual growth take place under the protective umbrella of the authority of the church. Hence, we stress that each person should try to find a group where they can grow and develop. Hosts and helpers are responsible for helping each person under their care to find such a group.

A MODEL FOR MINISTRY

As well as having values on which our ministry is based, it is important to have a model about which we are confident so that all the theory may be put into practice and not left simply as theory. Over the years on Alpha we have developed a model which is not the only way nor even necessarily the best way, but it is one which we have found God works through and is simple enough for anyone to use and to feel confident in doing so.

When we pray for individuals we do so ideally with a team of two or, at most, three. Sometimes, for example on the Sunday morning of the weekend on the Holy Spirit, there are so many people who want to be prayed for that there are not enough hosts and helpers to go around. On these occasions we may only have one person praying for each individual. If this is the case we make it an absolute rule that men should pray for men and women for women. Often during these times of prayer the Holy Spirit brings out aspects of people's lives which are very personal and intimate. Also, at these moments a very strong bond may be formed between the person praying and the one being prayed for, and if the person is of the opposite sex there is a danger of mis-understanding and a misreading of signals. If there is more than one person praying then at least one should be of the same sex as the person being prayed for.

At these prayer times one person should take the lead and should be seen to do so with the prayerful help of the others. If more than one person is attempting to lead there is a danger that signals will be confused. For example, it is not helpful if one is say-ing, 'Hold on,' and the other is saying, 'Let go!'

As far as possible it is good to find a relaxed and private place to pray. If there are a lot of people in the room, it is important that others around cannot hear everything that is being said, to avoid embarrassment for the person receiving prayer. In other situations, I have sometimes seen the most inappropriate raising of voices and even shouting, to the intense discomfort of the person receiving prayer.

We usually begin by asking the person what they would like prayer for. We then take time to sort out difficulties in under-standing, belief and assurance. Often there is a need for repen-tance and forgiveness, both receiving forgiveness and forgiving others. Lack of repentance and forgiveness is a major stumbling block to the work of the Holy Spirit in our lives.

Sometimes at this point it becomes clear that the person is not yet a Christian. Each member of the team needs to be confident that they can lead someone to Christ. I would usually go through the booklet *Why Jesus?* briefly and then ask the person if they would like to pray the prayer in the back right then or whether they would rather go away and think about it (it is important always to give people a let out which is equally acceptable so that they do not feel pressurised into doing something for which they are not ready). If they say they would like to do so right then, I would pray for them briefly and then encourage them to read the prayer out loud, slowly and thoughtfully, adding anything they wish. After this I would pray another prayer for them asking the Spirit of God to come and fill them.

Others may already be Christians but have never really experienced God or the power of the Holy Spirit. We need to encourage them with truth through scriptural illustrations and promises. We need to deal with any difficulties they may have. They may say, 'Am I quite ready?' to which the answer, in one sense, is that we will never be totally ready. Some say, 'I'm unworthy,' to which the answer is, 'We are all unworthy. That is why Jesus died for us.' Most often there is a feeling that it could 'never happen to me'. For example, they might want to receive the gift of tongues but say, 'I could never speak in another language.' Again, we need to raise faith by pointing to the promises of God (1 Corinthians 14:2, 4, 14; Matthew 7:11). One aspect of faith is taking a promise of God and daring to believe it.

As we pray for the person we stay facing them and, if they have no objection, we lay hands on them. Then, keeping our eyes open, we ask the Holy Spirit to come. We welcome him when we see signs of his working and wait on God as we pray for further directions. It is important not to pray 'around-the-world' prayers, ie going off in every conceivable direction because we are running out of things to pray. Rather we should silently ask God what he wants to do or say, how he wants to encourage the person and what gifts he wants to impart.

On the Alpha weekend we often pray for people to receive the gift of tongues (see *Alpha – Questions of Life*, pp 148–153). This is not because it is the most important gift but because the Alpha course is a beginners' course and the gift of tongues is a beginners' gift. It is neither the mark of being a Christian, nor a necessary sign of being filled with the Spirit. The gift of tongues does not elevate you into a spiritual elite, nor is it indeed necessary to speak in tongues. However, both in the Bible and in experience it is often the first obviously supernatural gift of the Spirit which people receive. Our understanding of the New Testament is that it is available to all Christians and therefore we can pray with great confidence for them to receive.

The small group is the place to deal with people's fears and hesitations. I would ask those in the small group if anyone has had any experience in this area, good or bad. If they have, I ask them to speak about it. Usually there is someone (it might be a host or a helper) who speaks in tongues themselves and is able to explain what it is and what the benefits are.

When praying for people to receive the gift of tongues I have found the greatest barrier is a psychological one – making the first sound. Once a person has made the first sound the rest usually follows quite naturally. In order to help people to get over this barrier I explain this difficulty and suggest that they start by copying what I or one of the other pray-ers is saying. Then I start to speak in tongues slowly so that they can follow. Once they have made the first sound they are usually away praying in their own language. I encourage them to try and concentrate on their relationship with God and try, as far as possible, not to be self-conscious. Rather they should concentrate on praising God with the new language he has given to them.

After we have finished praying for a person to be filled with the Spirit, receive a gift, be healed or whatever it is, we should ask what is happening and what they sense God is saying to them. We should encourage them to hold on to the promises of God, and warn them against possible increased temptation. We don't believe it is possible that 'nothing has happened'. They may not be aware especially at the time but when we ask the Spirit of God to come, he has promised to come. They may not know the difference until hours or even days later but something will have happened. We need to encourage them to keep in touch and to let us know how they are getting on. Of course, it is not a one-off experience; they need to go on being filled with the Spirit (Ephesians 5:18).

OPPORTUNITIES FOR MINISTRY

Much of the ministry takes place on the weekend away. The early part of the weekend is usually spent in raising faith and dealing with difficulties. On Friday night we have a very short talk on the Holy Spirit based around John 15:26. I try to keep this short and light-hearted as people are often exhausted after a busy week and a long journey.

On the Saturday morning we look at 'Who Is the Holy Spirit?' and 'What Does the Holy Spirit Do?' (see *Alpha – Questions of*

Life, Chapters 8 and 9). Then at 12.15 pm we go into the usual small groups and look at 1 Corinthians 12:1–8. This gives people an opportunity to discuss some of the most obviously supernatural gifts of the Spirit.

On Saturday afternoon there is an opportunity to ask for counselling with an experienced (though not professionally trained) counsellor. We put up a list of the counsellors and people can sign up for this if they have questions they want to ask, difficulties they would like help in thinking through, or if they would like to receive prayer for some area in their lives. During these sessions some give their lives to Christ, some are filled with the Spirit; others receive new gifts.

On the Saturday evening (at 5.00 pm) I speak on 'How Can I Be Filled with the Holy Spirit?' (Chapter 10 in *Alpha – Questions of Life*). At the end of the talk I explain that I am going to invite the Holy Spirit to come and fill those who would like to be filled and give the gift of tongues to those who would like to receive. I ask everyone to stand, to close their eyes and to hold out their hands in front of them if they would like to receive. Our body language often expresses what we feel, and holding out our hands is what we do when we are about to receive a gift: thus it is a sign between the person and God that they would like to receive.

I then pray a prayer which others can echo in their hearts. It is a prayer of repentance, faith and commitment to Jesus Christ. I then ask the Holy Spirit to come and fill all those who have invited him into their lives. We then wait and watch as he comes and does what he wants to do. It is always different and always exciting to see God at work in our midst. Sometimes the manifestations of the Spirit are obvious. Some are so overwhelmed by the Holy

Spirit they find it hard to remain standing. Others are so deeply moved by the love of God that tears run down their faces. Some are so filled with joy that they burst out laughing. For others there is no outward manifestation but a work of God in their hearts is bringing a sense of peace and a deep assurance of his presence and love. All should be encouraged, and no one should be made to feel guilty, second-rate or rushed along against their will.

At the end of the course I send out questionnaires asking (a) whether people were Christians before the course and (b) how they would describe themselves now. If there is a change I ask when that change occurred. For many the decisive moment is the Saturday evening of the weekend. Here are five examples of how people at one Alpha weekend described their experiences:

– 'After the talk about "How Can I Be Filled with the Holy Spirit?" we all stood up and the Holy Spirit came into the room. I knew that God was real so I asked Jesus into my heart and he's been there ever since . . . I have suddenly got a whole new outlook on life.'

– The change had occurred 'during the Saturday evening talks/services. I was filled with the Holy Spirit. I felt a white sheet wipe me clean then a strong rush of light came through me from my waist and up out of my head – the feeling made me lift my arms in the air.'

– 'I had been a Christian in my head only. This changed on the Alpha weekend when God spoke to me personally. I asked him for his Holy Spirit and the result was electrifying.'

– Someone who had been involved in the New Age movement at the start of the course said that the change occurred on the Saturday evening when 'the Spirit shook me from head to foot'.

– 'I had a phenomenal experience of the Holy Spirit cleansing me, freeing me, releasing my sins and loving me; giving me a fresh plateau, a new life. It was the 20 February when I really started to *live!*'

After the Saturday evening we respond to God in songs of thanksgiving and praise. Sometimes we will sing in tongues. I explain that singing in tongues together is different from all speaking in tongues together. Speaking in tongues without interpretation is a private activity which should only be done on our own. Singing in tongues is a corporate activity of praise and worship to God, co-ordinated by the Spirit of God. On occasions, it has been one of the most beautiful and almost angelic sounds I have ever heard. It is also a golden opportunity for people to receive the gift of tongues as they begin to sing praises to God in the language he gives them.

We do not usually pray for individuals on the Saturday night unless they specifically ask for prayer (which some often do at this stage). Instead, after supper we have an evening of entertainment organised by someone on the team. This is a good time for people to relax and unwind by performing or spectating. We invite participation by anyone who would like to contribute. It is usually a mixture of musical contributions, joke telling and amusing sketches. The quality is sometimes a little mixed, but it always involves lots of laughter. We try to ensure that the whole evening is as positive and upbuilding as possible.

On Sunday morning at 9.45 am we meet in small groups briefly to make sure that everyone is happy and to discuss any difficulties or questions which may have arisen on the Saturday, and at 10.30 am we have our informal communion service. We begin with praise and prayer. Then we have a talk on 'How Can I Make the Most of the Rest of My Life?' (see *Alpha – Questions of Life*, Chapter 15). At the end I invite people to give every part of their lives to God, 'to offer your bodies as living sacrifices' (Romans 12:1). This is the appropriate response to all that God has done for us. In some circles it would be described as a 'wholeheartedness talk'. It might be argued that this should come before the talk on being filled with the Spirit; that as we open all the doors of our house he fills each part with his Spirit. I am sure there is something in this, but the movement in Scripture is from him to us. He blesses us out of sheer grace and mercy and we respond by giving ourselves to him out of love. When we begin to understand and experience the love of God for us as we are filled with his Spirit, our only appropriate response is to give everything we have to him.

After the talk, we greet one another with a sign of peace. At this stage we have a few moments' break and move around greeting one another and chatting briefly. By this time there is a lot to talk and laugh about and there is usually quite a din! After the peace we sing a song of praise. We have an offering which covers the cost of those who could not afford to pay for all or part of the weekend. One of the exciting things about these weekends is that we almost always end up with exactly the amount in the offering to cover those we have subsidised. People are learning right from the start that in the Christian family those who have more should help those who have less.

I then explain the communion service (along the lines of *Alpha – Questions of Life*, pp 214–215). This is a good opportunity to teach about the central service of the Christian faith. Many comment on the beautiful simplicity and unity in this, and some experience God's love for the first time as they relax and receive the bread and wine.

After the communion is over I invite people to stand and again ask the Holy Spirit to come and work among us. After waiting for a short time I ask members of the team to begin praying with those who would like prayer. At this stage it is important for each member of the team to have the courage and confidence to go and pray for those in their groups along the lines I have suggested earlier in this chapter. This prayer goes on for some time. I usually end the service with a song and the blessing at around 1.00 pm, but prayer for some continues while the rest of us go to lunch.

After lunch at 2.00 pm we gather for five minutes to give thanks to our hosts and deal with any final administrative matters. We arrange to meet at the evening service (for those who are able to come), and reserve all the front seats of the church for those who have been on the weekend. For many it is their first time in the church. There is always a sense of great excitement and celebration on these occasions. The ministry of the Spirit continues and some are filled with the Spirit and receive gifts during or after the evening service.

Another excellent opportunity for those on the course to learn about ministry is the healing evening (*Alpha – Questions of Life*, Chapter 13) which occurs during week nine. The evening follows the normal pattern until after coffee at 9.00 pm. On this evening we do not then go into small groups: rather, we stay together for a practical healing session.

At this point we outline the model of healing prayer which we follow (*Alpha – Questions of Life*, pp 198–202). We then explain that God sometimes gives words of knowledge (1 Corinthians 12:8) which point out whom God wants us to pray for and which are also an aid to faith in this area. We have found that people receive these words in various ways. Some may get a mental picture of the part of the body which God wants to heal. Some will merely receive an impression, and others may sense that they hear or see words. We have found that one of the most common ways we receive words of knowledge is by what we call 'a sympathy pain': someone senses pain in their body, which they know is not really theirs.

Simon Dixon, who has since become our organist, had a stabbing pain when he moved or when he was touched around his jaw or neck. It had been very painful for a year and a half and he had been told it couldn't be cured. He had lots of medical tests, but the doctors did not know what was wrong. They thought it might be a brain tumour. He was finally diagnosed as having auricular neuralgia. He was on a lot of drugs and at times his vision was affected. A woman in our congregation called Emma had felt a pain in her jaw which she thought must be a sympathy pain and therefore a word of knowledge. As a result, after prayer for healing, he was sufficiently cured to come off the drugs and after further prayer was totally healed. Since then he has been perfectly healthy.

At the end of this explanation we ask if anyone senses that they have any words of knowledge. Usually there are many – often received by those who are relatively new Christians who have never had the disadvantage of being told that God does not speak to his people today. They expect God to speak to them and he does. We write down all the words of knowledge. Sometimes we go through the list one by one asking people to identify themselves (providing, of course, the condition described is not one likely to cause embarrassment). On other occasions we simply ask all those who want to respond to stand at the same time.

Next, we ask one of those who have responded (if they are willing) to be prayed for in public. We then get two or three experienced people to pray for the person to provide a model of how to pray for healing. Whoever is leading the evening explains exactly what is happening.

Then we arrange for two or three people to pray for each of those who have responded to the words of knowledge. We try to get those who have had the particular words of knowledge to pray for those who responded to them. By this time almost everyone on the course is involved in the ministry. If there are any not involved we suggest they join a group to watch and learn from what is going on.

It is very exciting to see those who have only recently come to Christ praying, often with great faith, for others in a similar position. We have seen some remarkable healings on these evenings and we nearly always see conversions as well. One teenager called Bill brought his mother Judy, who was not a Christian, on an Alpha course. She had enjoyed the course but was still quite sceptical about the healing evening. That night there was a word of knowledge for a shoulder injury. She responded and was healed. She said afterwards, 'Many things had happened to me during Alpha that were answers to prayer which I had tried to explain away as coincidences, but it was the healing that made me realise that I could no longer say it was a coincidence. I prayed in my heart and made a commitment.' Since then she has been a helper on a number of Alpha courses, being increasingly involved in the organisation and administration.

The ministry of the Spirit is crucial to Alpha – without it, it would not really be an Alpha course. We have found that time and again God has honoured simple requests for him to send his Spirit among us. Amazing and profound changes always occur in people's lives as a result. We are continuing to see people give their lives to Christ, be filled with the Spirit, get excited about Jesus and bring their friends to the next course.

Appendix A

Alpha Talk Scheme

The fifteen talks which make up the Alpha course are:

- Is There More to Life than This? (formerly *Christianity: Boring, Untrue and Irrelevant?*)
- Who Is Jesus?
- Why Did Jesus Die?
- How Can We Have Faith? (formerly *How Can I Be Sure of My Faith?*)
- Why and How Do I Pray?
- Why and How Should I Read the Bible?
- How Does God Guide us?
- An Introduction to the Weekend
- Who Is the Holy Spirit?
- What Does the Holy Spirit Do?
- How Can I Be Filled with the Holy Spirit?
- How Can I Resist Evil?
- Why and How Should I Tell Others?
- Does God Heal Today?

- What about the Church?
- How Can I Make the Most of the Rest of My Life?

Talk 1 is given at the celebration supper at the end of the course. Talks 8, 9, 10 and 15 are given at the weekend away. The best time for the weekend is half way through the course, but the date is flexible. If it comes later then the talk scheme needs to be adjusted accordingly. Whenever the weekend falls it is helpful to give Talk 11, 'How Can I Resist Evil?', directly afterwards even if it means the sequence of the talks changes slightly. This is because we have found this subject very relevant at this point.

Appendix B

Administration

by Philippa Pearson Miles

On an Alpha course there is a lot of hard work behind the scenes and every job is vitally important. We aim to get everything 100 per cent right. Guests who come on the course will see that every effort has been made and that everything is run in an efficient way.

Some of this chapter will only apply to larger courses, where the first thing the course leader should do is appoint an administrator.

SET A DATE

Make sure that your Alpha course does not overlap with anything that will keep people from coming, eg Christmas, Easter and summer holidays. Remember to allow enough time for the supper parties at the end of the course and the three training sessions. If you are doing a Daytime Alpha (see Appendix C) then tie in your course with the school term and include a break for half term. We suggest you do not book the weekend away over the half-term period.

Prepare brochure/letter

Prepare an attractive brochure with all the relevant details and feel free to reproduce the Alpha logo. Alternatively, produce a simple letter which sets out all the dates with a tear-off slip at the bottom. It is also possible to purchase Alpha Invitations on which you can print the details of your course.

Inviting your team

First, contact the home group leaders of the church and ask them to suggest people whom they know who would be good Alpha hosts and helpers. It is vital to get the right people (see Chapters 3 and 5). It is important to emphasise commitment to the course, because if the hosts are not consistent in coming then there is no reason why anybody else should come either.

Emphasise that their commitment is not just for ten weeks but also for three training nights, social evenings with their group, follow-up after the course has finished, getting members into a home group and integrating them into the church. Insist that all hosts and helpers come to the training sessions. If they are unable to come, ask them to watch the talk on DVD. Even if some of your team have helped on several Alpha courses, they should come to every training session of every course. Even if one of your hosts has been hosting small groups for twenty years or so, stress that Alpha small groups are very different. Ask the hosts and helpers to commit themselves to pray for every member of their group.

ARRANGING LEADERSHIP OF GROUPS

This can be a very long task, so allow plenty of time. Be firm with your team, emphasising that everyone should be willing to do anything from leading to washing-up.

Arrange groups primarily by age and think carefully about the dynamics of the group: the balance of characters, social backgrounds, professions etc. It is also good to select a team from the same home group so that there can be continuity for the guests after the course, though this may not always work in practice. It is better to put together a team who will work well with one another. If you can, try to allocate a specific person in each group to look after the administration for their group, preferably someone who is gifted in that area and who can definitely come to the administration/prayer meetings every week.

ADVERTISING

The most effective way of advertising an Alpha course is through the celebration supper at the end of the course. This provides an opportunity for guests to invite their friends to see what they have been doing for the last ten weeks. (The supper is discussed in more detail later on in this Appendix.)

The two Sundays prior to the beginning of the Alpha course should be designated 'Alpha Sundays'. At Holy Trinity Brompton the first Sunday is a regular service with a testimony and a slot advertising Alpha. The second Sunday is a guest service which is designed especially for church members to invite their friends and family. This service is low-key and the sermon is evangelistic and challenging. Again Alpha would be advertised and a testimony heard. Alpha brochures and complimentary copies of *Why Jesus?* are given to everyone at the end. An easily identifiable Alpha team is available afterwards to answer questions.

Suggested guest service timetable

6.30 pm	Welcome
6.35 pm	Praise and worship
6.50 pm	Prayers
6.55 pm	Description of Alpha and one or two testimonies from people who have just completed the last course. We would suggest that nothing else is promoted at this point.
7.05 pm	Hymn or song
7.10 pm	Reading
7.15 pm	Sermon
7.35 pm	Hymn or song
7.40 pm	Final prayer, blessing and offer of one-to-one prayer ministry

Other churches have found that an advertisement in the parish magazine is helpful. Another idea is to send personal invitations to people in your area.

Placing guests in groups

Often you will have very little information about your guests. From the application form you may only have their name, address, telephone number, an idea of their age and their hand-writing!

Remember that these are individuals. At Holy Trinity Brompton we pray over almost every single application and ask for guidance. If someone is not happy in their group, they might well not come back, so it is very important to get it right. If you feel there is a genuine reason (eg a large age gap from the rest of the group) why someone should move to a different group, do it in the first week otherwise it is disruptive for those in the old group as well as the new one.

If a guest is a friend of someone on the team, try to find out as much as possible about the guest which will help you to put them in the right group. Quite often, it is better not to put the guest in the same group as their friend who is helping as they often feel inhibited and unable to ask questions. Always put married couples in the same group unless specifically requested not to. Aim to arrange to do this task on the last day before the course starts. In this way last-minute applications will be on your list, allocated a group and will have a pre-printed label.

Venue

One of the features of Alpha is that the setting should be unchurchy. The ideal venue is a home, but when the church outgrows a home a venue with a welcoming atmosphere needs to be found. It can often be difficult to make a church hall look

FIRST NIGHT

welcoming. Use standard lamps instead of overhead strip lighting; provide flowers; cover unattractive trestle tables; make sure that the room is warm but not stuffy; arrange the chairs so that guests can eat together in their groups. Make sure that there is good lighting on the speaker and that everyone is able to hear. This may involve arranging a PA system. Make sure that there is somewhere for people to leave their coats and a secure place for briefcases, bags etc.

It is also useful to have signs for directions to lavatories, the book-stall and where groups are meeting – put up a plan if necessary.

FIRST NIGHT

Your welcoming team are going to be the first people your guests will see. Often they arrive with many preconceived ideas of what Christians are like, so when they are greeted by a 'normal' person they are often surprised and it is very important that their first impression is a good one.

Your welcomers will need an alphabetical list of guests with the name of their group hosts and the group number. They will need to know how many men and how many women are in each group. This is helpful when unexpected guests arrive and need to be placed very quickly in a group. Welcomers should know who the group hosts and helpers are, and have to hand a list and a plan of where the groups are meeting.

At the end of the first evening of the course all the hosts and helpers should meet together to discuss and review the evening.

Labels

Every person should have a label with their name and group number on. (Ensure that the names are spelled correctly – accuracy is very important.) Set up a table with labels in alphabetical order and delegate one or two people to hand them out. Alternatively, provide a pack/folder with ready-made labels for each group host. Give team members a different coloured label so that guests can know who they are and ask them any questions. Keep some spare labels and a list of unexpected guests so that they have a pre-prepared label for the following week. We have found it useful to continue labels until week three.

Runners

Depending on the size and venue of your course you will know at what stage you will need runners. You will need to choose a team of runners (ie those who take the guests from the door to the group) who are headed up by a strong leader. Keep a team of runners for the first three weeks. Don't use group hosts as they will need to be in their groups to greet people. Again, remember that first impressions are important. The runner must be alert to remember the name, group number and location of the group. The welcomer should introduce the guest to the runner who will take the guest to get a label and take them to their group and introduce them to their group host. Then they should return quickly to the main door. Obviously, welcomers and runners should be friendly, but not effusive, as this can overwhelm guests on the first night.

Address lists

We give each group a blank form for them to fill in names and addresses and contact telephone numbers. However, it must be stressed to all the guests that this is not so that they will be sent junk mail or be chased up by telephone when they don't come back to the course. These lists are then typed up and one copy is returned to the group host updated each week until the fourth week. This is so that lifts may be arranged and guests may be contacted if there is any problem. We do not give each member of the group a copy of the list – if they want to exchange addresses and telephone numbers this can be done within the group. If a guest rings the church office for a telephone number of another guest, we do not give details under any circumstances.

BOOKSTALL

There is a list of recommended books in the *Alpha Course Manual*. Ideally a bookstall should be open for the whole evening (except during the talk). Ensure that the previous weeks' talks are available on CD or DVD so that anyone who missed a session can watch or listen to it later.

TREASURER

The treasurer will need to keep the overall accounts. He or she will also need to put out some bowls for supper money and to count it at the end of every evening. Furthermore they will need to collect and count the weekend money and the supper party money.

WORSHIP LEADER

The worship leader needs to be responsible for any other musicians, the songbooks or OHP acetates, all the sound equipment and perhaps also the taping of the talks, and will need to make sure that the weekend away has a worship leader.

WEEKEND ADMINISTRATOR/ORGANISER

Each group should fill in a form for the weekend which should be circulated two or three weeks before the event. Include on the form details of the date, price, to whom cheques should be made payable and children's rates. Ask for information regarding special diets, vegetarian meals, requests to share and late arrivals. Try to get people to arrange their own lifts and transport within the groups. Make sure that everyone has a map and a programme for the weekend (see 'Structure').

* Liaise with the conference centre over:
    sheets
    towels
    soap
    special
    diets
    bookshop – check that they are happy for you to take your
        own stock
    communion wine
    PA system
    recording equipment
    OHPs
    sports facilities
    places for small groups to meet

* Arrange for someone to look after any children (encourage people to bring their children if they would like to).
* Arrange for someone to organise entertainment on the Saturday evening.
* Arrange for someone to organise sport or other events on Saturday afternoon.
* Arrange for counsellors for people to chat to on Saturday

afternoon.

* Remember to take a calculator.
* Remember to take songbooks.
* Remind guests to bring their *Alpha Course Manual* and their Bible and any sports equipment.
* Take spare Bibles and manuals.
* Remember to take baskets or bowls for the collection on Sunday morning for the bursary fund.
* Keep an up-to-date list of those coming and who has paid and who has not.
* Try to keep the price under £75. Alpha weekends often fill a conference centre and you are therefore in a strong position to negotiate a good price. See the *UK Christian Handbook* (published by the Christian Research Association) for a list of conference centres.
* For those who are unable to afford the full amount, ask them to pay whatever they feel they can afford. The collection on Sunday almost always covers the amount needed.
* Another possibility is to link with other churches in your area for a joint Alpha weekend. Your Alpha Adviser might be able to help you with organising this.
* Remember to buy a small present for the staff at the conference centre.
* Make a plan of where everyone is sleeping. Many centres will offer to do this for you, but experience would suggest it is better to do it yourself.

COURSE SUPPER – 7.00 PM

Supper is an important aspect of Alpha. People often feel more relaxed chatting over supper. Often people have commented that the food kept them coming back to Alpha, so it is worth keeping the food to a good standard!

Depending on the numbers expected, arrange for a different group to cook supper each week. You will know when you need a caterer (approx 120 +). (Make sure you have enough paper plates and cups, coffee cups, knives, forks, tea, coffee, squash, milk, biscuits etc.)

If you don't have a task force, the group who cooked should do the washing up and clearing up. Using disposables will keep this to a minimum.

If a group is doing the cooking, the cost can usually be kept to approximately £2.00 per head. Put out bowls at the serving points and reimburse whoever paid for the food. If you have a caterer, we suggest a charge of approximately £3.50 or ask people to pay whatever they feel they can afford. Some suggestions for Alpha meals would include simple pasta dishes, shepherds pie, chili con carne and pizza. Make sure you have a vegetarian alternative. Many recipes can be found in *The Alpha Course Cookbook*.

TASK FORCE

The purpose of the Alpha task force is to provide practical services for the Alpha course. In this way very few people from the course will be asked to help with the more mundane tasks and will therefore not be distracted from their enjoyment of Alpha. The task force is vital to ensure that the course will run smoothly. They should be welcome to listen to the talks and should be given as much encouragement as possible. Always cherish your task force! A key appointment is the task force co-ordinator, who allocates the different tasks and takes pastoral care of the team.

The task force should make sure that enough Bibles and manuals are available and are ready to be handed out if necessary. Every guest should have a free manual. Place a pile of Bibles under one of the chairs in the small group. In this way, guests are not daunted by seeing Bibles on every chair (at Holy Trinity, the NIV is used). The task force should be available to help with car-parking – an important job. (Don't forget that at the beginning of the course, those helping with the car park are the first people the guests will meet.) They also need to ensure that each group has enough chairs and that each group has a sign to identify itself. They should make sure there are spare chairs for latecomers and then at the end of the evening their job is to put away chairs. Furthermore, the task force should put on any urns or kettles and set up the coffee stations. Make sure that every member of the task force has a name badge.

The task force should also run a bookstall, displaying the books recommended in the *Alpha Course Manual.* These books are available through the Alpha stockist scheme operating in many Christian bookshops in the UK. Course leaders might find it helpful to become Book Agents, thereby qualifying for a discount on Alpha materials.

Alpha supper parties

For your first Alpha course, hold a supper party before the course starts, then hold one at the end of every course so that guests on the course can invite their friends. Appoint one person to co-ordinate and organise the supper party and print some attractive invitations. These should be available at week seven for guests to take to give to their friends. At the same time start collecting money for the parties. Everyone should pay for their guests as well as for themselves. Get a team together to set up the party and another for washing up and clearing up at the end. These should preferably be those who are not inviting friends. Do everything possible to create a good atmosphere. Make a table plan and try to use proper plates and glasses, etc. Put flowers, candles and napkins on the table. The talk should come during coffee.

Questionnaires

At week nine, give each guest on the course a questionnaire (see Appendix E). This will enable you to see what God has been doing in people's lives, and will help in planning the next course. At the same time, give the group hosts a questionnaire and ask them to fill in details about every single member of their group (take the names from the address lists even if guests have not completed the course). Ask them whether their group members completed the course and, if not, do they know the reason? Ask them if their group members are going to do *A Life Worth Living* and then whether they are going into a home group (ask them to specify which one). Bearing in mind the supper party and perhaps the guest service before the next course, ask who could give a good testimony. Ask who would be a good Alpha helper, and make sure that you remember to invite them to help on the next course.

Philippa Pearson Miles was the administrator of the Holy Trinity Brompton evening Alpha course from 1992 to 1996.

Appendix C

Daytime Courses

by Deirdre Hurst

Daytime Alpha is held on Wednesday mornings and was originally designed for those who were likely to find it easier to attend a course during the day rather than in the evening. There are obvious categories: people with young children, those who are self-employed or unemployed and those who would prefer not to venture out alone at night. In our experience this has generally been a group for women, but lately, we have successfully included several men.

The daytime Alpha course has proved as successful as the evening course as a means of evangelism. This course, with its appeal to both the head and the heart, has seen many people come into relationship with Christ – from those very far away from Christianity to those who have sat in pews in churches for much of their lives, but have not understood that the heart of the Christian faith is a relationship with Jesus. One team member, who had brought about twelve people from her own church to do the morning course at Holy Trinity Brompton, said to me at the end of the ten weeks that she had sat for years in the church with these people and none of them had moved in any real way towards conversion. Now, many had been converted during the course and they all wanted to go on to another course.

VALUES

The daytime Alpha course promotes the same values as the evening Alpha with some small differences of emphasis, resulting from the time of day we meet and particularly from the ministry of 'women to women'.

Anyone may come, at any stage of their life and from any background. As with the evening Alpha it is very important to make people feel welcome. We try to foster relationships in a relaxed atmosphere. Although we only have one lunch together as part of the course, it is very often a sign of the groups gelling together and friendships being formed when groups begin to arrange to have lunch together after the course is over.

Many women these days do some kind of course in the morning – art, history, languages etc – so we can encourage them to come and learn about the Christian faith. We also find that many, even those who are not Christians, have been crying out to God for their needs and those of their family (without knowing him or his power to change things). As a consequence, they readily understand about prayer and begin to pray together early in the course.

CHOOSING THE TEAM AND THE HELPERS

We have the same priorities as for an evening Alpha, choosing people who have vision for what the course can do and choosing new Christians who have a lot of friends who do not know Christ and training them to be helpers for the next course. We find it possible to have smaller groups with the daytime Alpha, maybe eight or even six, and we have two team members and one helper to each group.

Groups

Most tend to enjoy the groups more than anything else. They often come needing love, acceptance and forgiveness and they find it in their groups. Some come with damaged lives from abuse of all kinds. Many need a place of peace where they can learn to accept God's forgiveness for those things they have done of which they feel ashamed, and where they can learn to trust God and to forgive those who have hurt them. We try to put people of similar age together and possibly those who live near each other. We find in particular that mothers enjoy being with others who have children of a similar age, as it means they all have similar joys and problems.

Setting for daytime Alpha

As with evening Alpha, daytime Alpha probably works best meeting in a home but can work very well in a church hall or similar building, providing there is room for a creche.

Numbers

The course seems to work equally well whatever the numbers. We have done courses from twenty people to two hundred, with the Lord working in equal power in people's lives.

RESOURCES

You will need one copy of the *Alpha Course Manual* and some training manuals for the team. The training manual, although geared for an evening Alpha, can be used equally well for a morning Alpha, adapting Appendix II, which is concerned with evening timings. If you prefer to do the course by watching the DVDs then these can be supplied.

TASK FORCE

It is important to be well organised and to have someone from among the helpers who will organise the coffee for each morning, set out chairs, organise the creche and be responsible for arranging the lunch. There should also be a prayer task force from the team, who meet together for prayer half an hour before the morning begins. All the team will be committed to praying but with the timing of school runs and other morning commitments, it is not always possible for all the team to meet beforehand.

TIMING AND INVITATIONS

The timing for the mornings works as follows:

10.00 am	Coffee
10.20	Welcome
	Worship
10.30	Talk
11.15	Additional short coffee break
11.30	Groups

| 12.00 | Creche ends |
| 12.15 | Finish |

We suggest a letter or invitation card inviting people to join the morning Alpha course, telling them how long the course is to run and the timing of the morning. For example:

MORNING ALPHA
29 September – 8 December
We invite you to join the new
Morning Alpha course
beginning on
29 September
The course runs for ten weeks on a Wednesday morning at
—— from 10.00 am to 12 noon approx. The mornings
provide time for talks addressing key issues relating to the
Christian faith, followed by a break for coffee, then
discussion groups, with an opportunity to ask questions.
There will be a special half-day with lunch on
10 November. Further details later.

The course is ideal for anyone who wants to learn more
about the Christian faith and/or anyone who would like to
enquire into what Christianity really means. It is a
wonderful opportunity to meet new people and make new
friends. There are creche facilities if you need them.

We do not have a weekend away as part of our daytime course but rather fit in a half-day on the power and work of the Holy Spirit as part of the regular weekly programme. This enables everyone to have an opportunity to hear about the Holy Spirit without having to break up their family routine for the weekend away. However if you belong to a church that offers a weekend away as part of its evening courses, the daytime guests could join in. This will give double the opportunity to hear about the Holy Spirit.

Suggested Alpha Holy Spirit Day

9.45	Coffee
10.00	Worship
10.15	Combined talk: 'Who Is the Holy Spirit?' & 'What Does the Holy Spirit Do?'
11.00	Coffee break
11.15	Small group discussions (1 Corinthians 12)
11.55	Worship: Two songs
12.00	Talk: 'How Can I Be Filled with the Holy Spirit?'
12.40	Ministry with worship
1.10	Lunch
2.00	Feedback in small groups
2.30	Finish

Daytime Alpha supper

The supper party at the end of the course is an excellent setting for married women to bring their husbands who, as we have found many times, have been very pleasantly surprised at some of the changes in the lives of their spouses, and it gives them a wonderful opportunity to hear the gospel in a relaxed environment. It has been one of the striking features of daytime Alpha that many of the husbands have gone on to do an evening Alpha and been converted to Christ. Of course, we do have many women on the course who are not married and they are more than welcome to bring their friends to the supper party.

THE RESULTS OF DAYTIME ALPHA

During the seven years that we have had a daytime Alpha, we have had many wonderful conversions and healings. We have often found that after only a few weeks of the course whole families are coming to church.

Deirdre Hurst has been running daytime Alpha at Holy Trinity Brompton since 1991. She has also helped at many conferences both in the UK and abroad.

Appendix D

Lunchtime Alpha Courses

Lunchtime Alpha courses have also been popular in recent years, many of them hosted by an existing Christian group in a firm or office. There are obvious time limitations, as a lunch break is generally no more than one hour long, but nevertheless people are coming to Christ on these courses. It is possible to adapt the timings to fit into one hour, using live speakers who reduce the material to its essential/key points and speak for twenty minutes only.

TWO POSSIBLE TIMINGS

One hour

12.30	Introduction, coffee and sandwich lunch
12.45	Shorter talk or use the *Alpha Express* DVD
1.10	Small groups/discussion
1.30	Finish

One-and-a-half hours

12.30	Light lunch
12.45	Notices and introduction

1.00	Talk
1.30	Small groups
2.00	Finish (with possibility of people lingering behind to talk)

Appendix E

Questionnaire

Name

Group

1. How did you hear about the Alpha course? Did you come to an Alpha supper party?

2. Why did you decide to do Alpha?

3. How many sessions did you attend?

4. (a)   (i) Were you a Christian when you started the course?
        (ii) Were you a regular churchgoer when you started the course?

   (b) How would you describe yourself now (in terms of the Christian faith)?

   (c) If the answers to (a) and (b) are different, when and how did the change occur?

5. In what ways, if any, did you benefit from doing the Alpha course?

6. What did you enjoy most about Alpha?

7. What did you find most difficult?

8. (a) Which, if any, CDs / DVDs did you buy?

   (b) Which, if any, books did you buy?

   (c) Did you find them helpful and if so why?
   (Please name any books or tapes which you found particularly helpful)

9. In what way could the course be improved?

   (a) Talks

   (b) Small groups

   (c) Generally

10. Any other comments

Appendix F

How to Avoid the Seven Common Mistakes

Research has revealed seven common mistakes that people make when running an Alpha course, which can prevent it from being a truly effective form of evangelism. The way to avoid these mistakes is to follow the seven key steps outlined below.

1. AIM TO ATTEND AN ALPHA CONFERENCE

Running Alpha without attending a conference is like driving a car without taking any lessons. We have found that those churches whose course leaders attend a conference experience a far higher degree of success with their Alpha course.

It may be that the Alpha course leaders who first made the decision to run Alpha in your church have now handed the responsibility to others. In this case, the new team will benefit from attending an Alpha conference. The aims of the Alpha conference are as follows:

a) To explain the theological and practical reasons for running Alpha

b) To share with others what we have learnt over the last twenty years from our own mistakes
c) To provide all the practical training needed to run an effective Alpha course
d) To consider the importance of:

- worship
- services
- talks (including a model Alpha evening)
- prayer ministry
- small group training

e) To provide opportunities for prayer ministry

If you have never been to a conference, we would be delighted if you would consider attending the next Alpha conference in your area or one of the two conferences held at Holy Trinity Brompton each year. Most course leaders have found it valuable to bring their leadership team with them to establish a sense of unity in purpose and vision. Details of Alpha conferences can be found in *Alpha News* or on the Alpha website: alpha.org. (If for some reason you are unable to attend a conference, the *How to Run the Alpha Course* DVD set is available.)

2. THINK ABOUT YOUR TEAM CAREFULLY

It is vital to get the right people hosting and helping on your Alpha course. The right team transforms a course and directly affects the number of guests attending Alpha.

What makes the right team?

Hosts and helpers on Alpha should be positive outgoing people who relate well to those outside the church. There is a simple test for good hosts and helpers. Ask yourself: 'Would I happily put my closest friend who is not a Christian in that person's group?'

How to avoid burnout

Keep renewing your Alpha team. It is important to keep an eye out for new people you can invite to join your team. Guests from your last course often make very good helpers and their faith is likely to grow as they help in a group. Those most reluctant to be helpers can be the best ones, as they identify well with new guests. Even those relatively new to the faith can make excellent group hosts. Always be looking for potential hosts in your congregation.

Remember to delegate to your team

Look out for other people's gifts and don't be afraid to use them. This will prevent you from becoming exhausted and will enable them to develop their talents. Some people are natural group hosts. Others love to serve by cooking, setting up, welcoming and so on. These are the people best suited to join the taskforce for your course. In larger courses the taskforce might even form their own small group.

3. STAY IN TRAINING

Alpha team training

Hosting an Alpha group is very different from leading any other type of church small group. On Alpha the emphasis is on group discussions and participation rather than playing the role of 'teacher'. The host acts more as a 'facilitator'.

The Alpha Team Training consists of three talks: 'Hosting Small Groups', 'Pastoral Care' and 'Prayer Ministry'. The first two training sessions should be held on the two weeks prior to the start of the course. We meet at 7.00 pm for supper so that the team can get to know each other before the course begins. We move on to worship and prayer at 7.45 pm. All the way through we stress the importance of praying for the course. We then have a talk and an opportunity to ask questions relating to the talk or any other aspect of the course. We then cover administrative details and recommended reading before the start of the course (*Alpha – Questions of Life*) and aim to finish by 9.30 pm. The ministry training session takes place during the week before the weekend away and follows the same format. These three talks are available on DVD, and a manual is also available. We also recommend that the team reads *Searching Issues* and *How to Run the Alpha Course – Telling Others*.

It is essential that you train each member of your Alpha team every time you run the course. Even those who have led on Alpha before will find it valuable, both to refresh their memory and to meet others who are helping on that course. The sessions also provide an opportunity to pray for the course.

The principles of Alpha

Experience shows that it is vital for teams to understand not just the 'whats' and 'hows', but also the 'whys' of Alpha – the principles of the course. The ideal way to achieve this is to take the core members of your team to an Alpha conference, which covers both the principles and the practicalities of the Alpha course. However, if this is not possible, consider showing the *How to Run the Alpha Course* DVD (which covers the talks on principles and practicalities) to your team once a year.

4. Follow the recipe

Alpha is tried and tested and it has been running in a wide range of settings for more than twenty years. Every ingredient has been included for a very important reason. Those courses that leave out one ingredient, such as the meal, diminish the impact of Alpha.

For example:

- The meal is an essential element, enabling guests to relax, friendships to form and groups to gel.
- The weekend or day away allows guests to look at the person and work of the Holy Spirit in a relaxed setting, giving them time to think through what they have heard or experienced.
- It is vital to give the guests the opportunity to respond and to be ministered to during the weekend.
- The healing night is a time when amazing things often happen. We have found that people are often more open to the Holy Spirit at this point than they are at the weekend.
- Including worship week by week helps to prepare the guests for the weekend. Some churches have found it helpful to use CDs because they do not have musicians.

5. Don't forget the weekend away

We highly recommend a weekend away. However, if only a day away is possible, that too will be effective. It is important to have one or the other and not to miss out the talks on the person and work of the Holy Spirit.

A survey carried out by the Methodist Church found a direct correlation between churches that left out the talks on the Holy Spirit and those that were disappointed with their Alpha course. The work of the Holy Spirit is crucial to Alpha and giving the guests an opportunity to be prayed for is a vital part of the course. Time and again God has honoured simple requests for him to send his Spirit among us – with profound changes often occurring in people's lives as a result. It is only through the work of the Spirit that we are able to see people give their lives to Christ, be filled with the Spirit, get excited about Jesus and bring their friends to the next course.

If you need any help with your weekend or day away, contact your Alpha Adviser, who can give advice or even arrange for a team to come and help you. (There is a list of Alpha Advisers in *Alpha News*.) You might also consider running an Alpha weekend or day away with other churches in your area.

6. Invite people from outside the church

Experience has shown that most of the guests on the first Alpha course run by a church are from the congregation. The second course may well be smaller, and again the majority of guests may be congregation members. By the third course there will be far fewer congregation members (as most of those interested will have come on the first or second course), there will probably be one or two guests from outside the church. That's fantastic because Alpha is primarily designed for non-churchgoers. The more non-Christians you have on your course, the more comfortable your guests will feel about exploring the Christian faith. The important thing is for the congregation to keep inviting their friends to Alpha, this keeps the balance tipped towards those outside the church with guests often inviting their friends, family and colleagues to the next course, thus further widening the pool of guests.

7. Keep Alpha rolling

Alpha is a long-term strategy which, when run well over an extended period, leads to a constant stream of new people. Experience has shown that churches who persevere with running Alpha three times a year in this way, even when their numbers on the course are reducing, find that they experience growth in the longer term.

Appendix G

Prayer and Alpha

PRAYER

Pastor Dutch Sheets wrote: 'Evangelism without prayer is like a grenade without a detonator. Prayer without evangelism is like a detonator without a grenade.' Prayer lies at the heart of the success of any Alpha course and many churches have testified to the dramatic improvement in the success of their course when they have started to pray for it. There are five situations where praying for Alpha is particularly appropriate.

1. Hosts and helpers pray for the individuals in their small group

As well as committing to the ten weeks of the Alpha course and the weekend away, the Alpha hosts and helpers are responsible for praying regularly for the guests in their group, ideally daily during personal prayer time. We recommend that two hosts and two helpers are recruited to look after eight guests, so each host and helper may like to take responsibility for praying for two guests. The hosts and helpers are in the best position to pray as they are aware of the needs of each individual as the Alpha course progresses.

2. Hosts and helpers pray together for their small group

In addition, the hosts and helpers of each small group can meet together, maybe before church on Sunday or some other suitable time, to pray for the course. This will help to unite the leadership team of the small group and to reinforce the individual prayer referred to above.

3. Hosts and helpers pray together immediately prior to the course

It is helpful for the whole Alpha team to meet each week before the guests arrive for a team briefing and prayer meeting. The items for prayer are largely self-defining, eg the weekend away, the Alpha celebration suppers, etc. This is particularly important for the session 'Does God Heal Today?', as the team can wait on the Lord for words of knowledge, pictures and so on. These can then be read out after the talk and people who respond to them can be offered prayer.

4. Prayer in Week 4 'Why and How Do I Pray?'

During the session 'Why and How Do I Pray?' guests are given a theology, model and practice for prayer. This relates primarily to personal prayer, which is a good starting point as people come into relationship with God. As prayer establishes itself in people's lives it should be possible to start praying together in the small group. Do not try to introduce prayer to the small group until the end of this session at the earliest. You may find that your group is not ready to pray together until after the sessions on the Holy Spirit. If possible try to pray together at least once prior to the talk 'Does God Heal Today?'

Tips for praying together in the small groups Don't rush this! Be sensitive to where people are spiritually. If you are going to open the session in prayer then we suggest saying something like, 'I have asked John to open in prayer' so that the other guests will not be afraid that the host might ask them to pray without giving notice at some time in the future. Remember that praying out loud for the first time can be quite an intimidating experience.

When you feel that the group is ready to pray, suggest that the group splits into triplets of all men or all women to pray. This makes it easier for people. The faith of the small group can be built up by feeding back answers to prayer.

When you start to pray in the small group, don't pray your longest and most eloquent prayer. The guests will feel that they could never do that – and then they won't! Pray a short, simple prayer and the guest will be encouraged to think, 'Well I could do better than that' – and then they will!

One of the hosts or helpers should refrain from praying, showing the group that it is all right not to pray aloud.

5. Praying for Alpha as a church

While it is important that those who are hosting and helping on Alpha are praying for the course, we also try to encourage the whole church to pray for the Alpha course. We have found that an open corporate prayer meeting held weekly on a different day to the Alpha course works well. The agenda covers all areas of the life of the church, but one of the regular items is prayer for evangelism and Alpha. This weekly prayer meeting is an integral part of church life and incorporates times of worship.

Anna Davies has run a number of Alpha courses in Weston-super-Mare. She writes: 'We had put a lot of effort into trying to run the past few Alpha courses really well but had seen very little come of it by way of new Christians being born. However, the prayer meetings, which began nine months ago, have provided an opportunity for more united, consistent prayer for Alpha and we are now seeing on this present Alpha course a significant change. Nearly every one of the twenty-four people on the course is not a Christian and there is an atmosphere of genuine openness to the gospel. We are aware of God being more present in a way that he has not been before and, very importantly, he seems to be peeling off some of the things in our own lives that hinder us from being effective communicators of the gospel.'

For more information on running a corporate prayer meeting, including a theology and a model for dynamic corporate prayer, please refer to *The Church on its Knees* by Jeremy Jennings and the *Prayer and Alpha* DVD.

Appendix H

Worship on Alpha

'Speak to one another with psalms, hymns and spiritual songs. Sing and make music in your heart to the Lord, always giving thanks to God the Father for everything, in the name of our Lord Jesus Christ' (Ephesians 5:19–20).

THE PRACTICALITIES OF INTRODUCING WORSHIP ON THE ALPHA COURSE

1. Why is worship an integral part of the Alpha course?
Worship is at the heart of a relationship with God. Men and women have been created by him to worship, whether they choose to do so or not. We are encouraged to worship God with the whole of our lives (Romans 12:1). Any practical introduction to the Christian faith must include teaching about worshipping God. The Alpha course does this by helping the guests to experience it first-hand.

Music plays a significant part in worship. Throughout the Bible, we are encouraged to express our worship, especially corporately, by using our voices and by playing instruments. When we worship we experience God's presence (Psalm 145:18, 2 Chronicles 5:13–14) and people may be converted (cf. Acts 16:25–30, Psalm 40:3).

Throughout Alpha, guests are invited to participate in worship by singing with a worship leader and, ultimately, by putting their trust in Jesus Christ. The last talk on the weekend away stresses the need to give the whole of our lives to God. Corporately, this giving of ourselves may be expressed through the times of worship on each evening of the course.

These times will be referred to as 'the worship' and may be seen as complementary to worshipping God with every breath that we have.

2. The experience of worship on Alpha

Although at the beginning many find the worship the most difficult part of Alpha, by the end it is generally the most appreciated time.

One guest who wasn't a Christian at the beginning of the course said, 'The singing on the first night was terrifying.' Yet by the end of the course, when asked what was most enjoyed, he said, 'The singing – I feel like my voice has a purpose! I hardly ever got the chance to sing before. It's great to sing and really mean the words.'

Why is it so difficult? Most people in today's culture do not sing very often, apart from perhaps in the shower or at a football match. It is therefore a little optimistic to expect uninhibited praise on the first night. It is important not to compound the situation further by singing personal statements of faith (ie, songs which express personal experience such as 'I Love You Lord') too early in the course. For those who are wary of singing in public, it is even more difficult to sing something they do not believe.

In today's culture, there is unfortunately a perceived stigma attached to some church music. It is seen as out of date, boring or embarrassing. Many come to church for the first time with this perception in the back of their mind. If we are going to use worship on Alpha, it is important to challenge this perception and prove it wrong. As with everything else on the course we have tried to follow the maxim: 'Strive for excellence or don't do it at all.'

Why is it so appreciated? As guests find faith, worshipping God becomes a natural desire. Music is a wonderful expression of this desire.

Part of the vision for Alpha is to demonstrate what church is like. Worship music is an aspect of typical church life. Learning how to worship God and being familiar with the hymns and songs that we usually sing helps guests to integrate into our church at the end of the course. Worship becomes for many a first experience of communicating with God. It helps to develop an understanding of what God is like: real, awesome, loving and approachable.

3. How to do it

Although worship should always be Christ-centred, we try to bear in mind that the Alpha course as a whole is a ministry to the guest. Therefore we aim to introduce worship both gradually and sensitively. Here are a few pointers which might help.

Time. On the first night, we sing two songs, which lasts about five minutes. For the first few weeks the time of worship is kept short to enable guests to get used to singing. An extra song may be added as appropriate. At the weekend, guests are encouraged to worship for longer, with up to five or six songs at each session. As guests find faith, their enthusiasm for worship seems to increase, and times of worship lasting twenty minutes become the norm for the rest of the course.

Song choice. There is a suggested song list at the end of this Appendix. In addition, you may like to use other hymns and songs which you already use in your church.

Song choice should initially favour objective truth: songs of universal fact about the unchanging all-powerful nature of God. Sensitivity to unbelieving guests will lead to the avoidance, early in the course, of such songs as 'I Believe in Jesus' or 'I Love You Lord'. These songs presume faith and must be owned before they can be sung with integrity. As guests begin to allow God to integrate objective truth and personal experience, so worship times will begin to reflect their deepening faith and intimacy with God.

Be sure to have the correct copyright licences for using songs on sheets or overhead projector (OHP) transparencies. Details are given at the end of this Appendix.

What to expect on the night. Initially, many in the group will not sing, and those who do will probably not sing very loudly. It can therefore feel uncomfortable for those leading. I always try to keep these things in mind:

- Don't worry if it feels like a performance. Truth is being sung whether the congregation joins in or not (cf. Isaiah 55:10–11).
- Be patient. Consider what it must be like for the newcomer.

There is plenty of time for what you may consider true worship to develop.

- A key governing principle of the Alpha course as a whole is the respect for the individual (see 1 Peter 3:15). Don't force anyone to do anything with which they may feel uncomfortable. Rather say, 'Please just be yourself, stand or sit, sing or don't sing; do whatever you feel like.' Emphasise the scriptural encouragement to 'make music in your heart' (Ephesians 5:19) which is where true worship lies.

- Encourage every team member and host to be sensitive and to moderate their worshipping fervour! The whole Alpha evening, and therefore the time of worship, is primarily a ministry to the guest not the host or helper. It is vital that the guests feel as comfortable as possible and are not distracted by what they might consider unusual actions on the part of the hosts and helpers.

- Clapping, raising hands, using percussion, and other such activities are difficult for many at first because they appear to be odd behaviour. If and when these elements are introduced, explain why they're done – they're not part of some bizarre ritual, but rooted in Scripture.
  - Clapping and shouting – Psalm 47:1
  - Dancing, tambourine and instruments – Psalm 150
  - Lifting hands – 1 Timothy 2:8; Psalm 63:4; Lamentations 3:41

Having said all of this, the authentic worship of the team is vital and often touches the guests as they witness a genuine enjoyment of worshipping God.

4. Alpha worship leaders: characteristics and skills

We have always appointed a worship leader to take responsibility for the music on the course. We have found it helpful to pray for the right person to lead, taking into account, where possible, the following characteristics:

A desire to worship God. The ruling passion in any worship leader's heart should be to enjoy worshipping God, both individually and in the church context. This desire then overflows into the leadership of others so that they too may enjoy God in this way.

A lifestyle of worship. 'The Lord does not look at the things people look at. Human beings look at the outward appearance, but the Lord looks at the heart' (1 Samuel 16:7). Worship is about the whole of our lives being orientated towards God. Our motives and actions must match up to the sentiments expressed in the songs.

A servant heart. Any ministry is one of service – serving God, the body of Christ and those in authority. It is vital that the worship leader is open to ideas, suggestions and, if necessary, correction. Humility is the key to successful leadership (see Mark 10:43–45).

Musical ability. The following points are things to aim for if you are selecting a worship leader:

- He or she should ideally be able to play a 'lead' instrument, eg guitar or piano, to a reasonable standard. If they do not, they should have a close rapport with a guitarist or pianist so that the music gives a clear lead to the guests.

- It is helpful for the leader to have a strong singing voice with good intonation.
- Even and consistent rhythmic ability is essential.
- They should aim to have a thorough knowledge of the songs and their various styles.
- A professional background in music can sometimes be a hindrance rather than a help as a worship leader is not a performer. In fact, he or she needs to be full of humility, willing to decrease and let Jesus increase (John 3:30).
- If there are a number of musicians, time should be taken to arrange songs in rehearsals ahead of time.
- An eye for detail is useful, eg ensuring that song-books, chordsheets and OHP transparencies are all available; that all the instruments are in tune; that the musicians' area is tidy. This inspires confidence in the musicians and the guests.
- Full preparation, practice and prayer will free the leader and the guests to be relaxed.

Musical attitude

- The worship leader should keep his or her eyes open during the songs. Eye contact encourages the guests and enables the leader to see the extent to which they are involved in worshipping.
- Smile. It is a wonderful privilege and joy to worship God.
- Only the worship leader leads the worship. Prayerfully work out the song list beforehand, stick to it and don't be subject to having to sing the favourite songs of individuals. It's a good thing, and far from unholy or 'Spirit-quenching', to plan ahead.

- The worship leader only leads the worship! Just play and sing the songs. Do not stop between songs to give mini sermons. Let it flow.

ALPHA SUGGESTED SONG LIST

It must be stressed that the songs listed below are only ideas. Feel free to experiment and find what works best for you.

Week 1	O Lord My God How Great is Our God
Week 2	Amazing Grace How Great is Our God
Week 3	O Lord My God Everlasting God
Week 4	Everlasting God I Stand Amazed
Week 5	How Great is Our God I Stand Amazed
Week 6	Mighty to Save When I Survey
Week 7	O Lord My God Mighty to Save

Weekend Away	O Lord My God
	Happy Day
	Blessed be Your Name
	Love Came Down
	Mighty to Save
	How Great is Our God
	The Stand
	This is Our God
	This is My Desire
	I Stand Amazed
	Remain
	When I Survey
	All Glory
	Glory in the Highest
	Faithful One
Week 8	Blessed be Your Name
	How Great is Our God
	Here I Am to Worship
Week 9	O Lord My God
	Mighty to Save
	When I Survey
Week 10	Everlasting God
	This is Our God
	I Stand Amazed
Week 11	Blessed be Your Name
	Everlasting God
	Amazing Grace

Copyright licence details

If you wish to make OHP transparencies of your own or copy or print songsheets, you must have a CCL licence. This may be obtained from:

Christian Copyright Licensing Ltd
PO Box 1339
Eastbourne
BN21 4YF
Tel: 01323 417711

USA
CCLI
17201 NE Sacramento Street
Portland
Oregon 97230
Tel: 503 257 2230
Fax: 503 257 2244

South Africa
CCL Africa
PO Box 2347
South Africa
Tel: 21 975 1393

Australia/New Zealand
CCL Asia Pacific
PO Box 1254
Castle Hill
New South Wales 2154
Australia
Tel: 2 894 5386

Scandinavia
c/o Copycare Scandinavia AB
Glammelgardsvagen 38–42
S–112 64 Stockholm
Sweden
Tel: 0 861 800 30

Appendix I

Alpha Weekend Entertainment

ORGANISER'S INSTRUCTIONS

The entertainment is a crucial part of the Alpha weekend and is a great way of breaking down barriers and unifying the group. However, it is also a potential disaster area if it goes on too long or if some of the material is inappropriate.

The role of the organiser of the entertainment is to raise everyone's enthusiasm for the entertainment, encouraging people/groups to contribute acts and to collect the acts, ensuring that each act is in line with the pointers below. It sometimes takes a lot of tact to deal with difficult people who want to do an act which may be unsuitable. It is important to be kind but firm. The last part of the job is to compere the evening – linking up all the acts and rallying the audience.

Here are some pointers to help the evening go smoothly:

1. There should be nothing religious.
2. There should be nothing with unhelpful innuendo.
3. There should be no in-jokes.

4. We suggest about ten acts/sketches/musical pieces in total.
5. The entertainment should last for no longer than one hour in total.
6. Begin at 9.00 pm and end before 10.00 pm.
7. Keep a record of any acts that you thought worked particularly well, for possible future use.
8. If you have any problems or doubts always ask the administrator or the leader of the weekend.

Notes

1. *The Daily Mail,* 13 January 2004.
2. From the Church of England website, 13 January 2004: www.cofe.anglican.org
3. Statistics from *1992 Social Trends* from the Central Statistical Office.
4. Leading missiologist David Bosch defines evangelism as the proclamation of salvation in Christ to those who do not believe in him, calling them to repentance and conversion, announcing forgiveness of sin, inviting them to become living members of Christ's earthly community and to begin a life of service to others in the power of the Holy Spirit.
5. John Stott, *The Contemporary Christian* (IVP, 1992), p241.
6. Pope Paul VI in *Evangelii Nuntianti Apostolic Exaltation on Evangelisation in the Modern World.*
7. Michael Green, *Evangelism through the Local Church* (Hodder & Stoughton, 1990), pix.
8. John Stott, *The Contemporary Christian* (IVP, 1992), pp121, 127.
9. Graham Tomlin, in R. T. France and A. E. McGrath (eds), *Evangelical Anglicans* (SPCK, 1993), pp82–95.
10. John Stott, *Issues Facing Christians Today* (Marshalls, 1984), pxi.
11. Lesslie Newbigin, *The Open Secret* (SPCK, 1995), p11.

12. Wayne Grudem, *Systematic Theology* (IVP, 1994), pp763–787.

13. David Pawson, *Fourth Wave* (Hodder & Stoughton, 1993), pp36–37.

14. John Pollock, *John Wesley* (Hodder & Stoughton, 1989), p118.

15. George Whitefield's *Journal* (Banner of Truth, 1992).

16. Charles Finney, *Memoirs of Rev. Charles G. Finney* (Fleming H. Revell, 1876), p19.

17. John Pollock, *Moody without Sankey* (Hodder & Stoughton, 1963), pp83, 87.

18. R. A. Torrey, *The Baptism with the Holy Spirit* (Dimension Books, 1972), pp11, 54.

19. John Pollock, *Billy Graham* (Hodder & Stoughton, 1966), pp62–63.

20. *The Word Among Us*, daily meditations for May 1996, 'A Pentecost Retreat with Fr. Raniero Cantalamessa, Preacher to the Papal Household'.

21. Robert W. Jenson, *Systematic Theology*, vol. 2, *The Works of God* (Oxford University Press, 1999) p.185, cited by Colin Gunton, *The Christian Faith* (Blackwell Publishers, 2002) p9.

22. Nicky Gumbel, *Alpha – Questions of Life* (Kingsway, 1993).

23. Nicky Gumbel, *Why Jesus?* (Kingsway, 1991).

24. Juan Carlos Ortiz, quoted in *Alpha* Magazine, January 1993.

25. R. A. Torrey, *Personal Work* (Pickering & Inglis, 1974), pp9–10.

26. Nicky Gumbel, *Searching Issues* (Kingsway, 1994).

27. *Church Times*, 7th September 1989.

28. C. H. Spurgeon, *Lectures to My Students* (Marshall Pickering, 1954), p77.

29. Phillips Brooks, *Lectures on Preaching: The Yale Lectures* (Dutton, 1877; Allenson, 1895; Baker, 1969), p28.

30. *The New Bible Dictionary* (InterVarsity Press, 1962), p827.

Also by Nicky Gumbel:

Is God a Delusion?

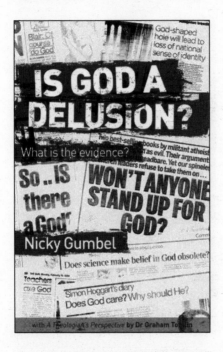

Drawing upon his experience as a barrister, Nicky Gumbel addresses the biggest issue of our age: does God exist?

(Book/Code 9781905887194 /£4.99)

Alpha –
Questions of Life

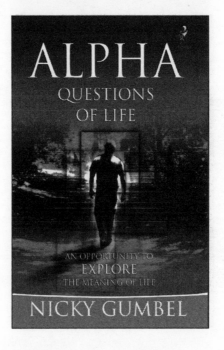

The Alpha course talks in book
form

(Book / Code HTB04 / Trade Code
9781842911648 / £6.99)

A Life Worth Living

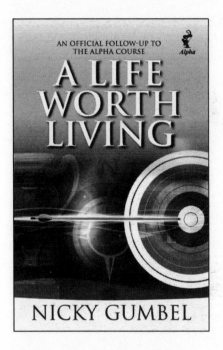

Based on Paul's letter to the Philippians, this book offers a practical and positive guide to achieving exactly this

(Book / Code HTB09 / Trade Code 9780854767403 / £6.99)

Searching Issues

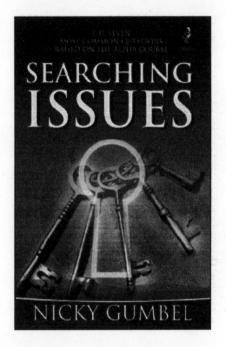

Tackles the seven most common
objections to the Christian faith

(Book / Code HTB05 / Trade Code
9780854767397 / £6.99)

Challenging
Lifestyle

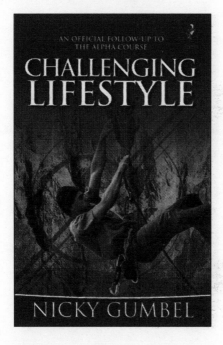

Examines the Sermon on the
Mount and presents us with some
radical alternatives for how to live
in the 21st century

(Book / Code HTB46 / Trade Code
9780854767427 / £6.99)

The Heart of
Revival

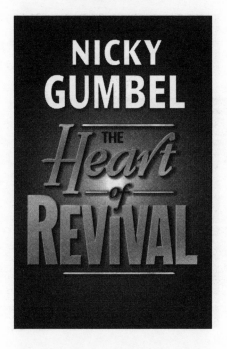

Based on Isaiah, Nicky Gumbel
draws out some important truths
by interpreting what revival might
mean and how we can prepare to
be a part of it

(Book / Code HTB89 / Trade Code
9780854767564 / £6.99)

30 Days

A thirty day practical introduction to reading the Bible

An excellent introduction to reading
the Bible, designed to be read over
thirty days

(Booklet / Code 9781902750811 / £2.50)

The Alpha Course

The Alpha course is a practical introduction to the Christian faith initiated by Holy Trinity Brompton in London, and now being run by thousands of churches, of many denominations, throughout the world.

For more information about Alpha, and related ministries such as The Marriage Course and The Marriage Preparation Course, please see:

alphafriends.org

Or contact:

Alpha International
Holy Trinity Brompton
Brompton Road
London SW7 1JA
Tel: 0845 644 7544
Email: info@alpha.org

If you would like a copy of the Alpha Publications Brochure, outlining details of resources available for purchase, or to order course materials, please contact the **Alpha Publications Hotline** on:

Tel: 0845 758 1278

Or visit: alphashop.org

To order from overseas:
Tel: +44 1228 611749

Alpha